MW01289021

DO THESE WORK BOOTS MAKE MY FEET LOOK FAT?

By Kathleen A. McLaughlin

ISBN 978-1-4949080-7-2

First Printing – January 2014

Printed in the United States of America

Introduction

The 1970's was a stimulating time for women in the workplace. In 1972, I obtained a job with San Diego Gas & Electric as the first woman auto mechanic's helper. The pay was good - the communal atmosphere was not. This book is a collection of snippets of my non-traditional life: personal time, work time and my promotion into the curious world of corporate administration. I amusingly introduce you to the challenges, the people and the triumphs. The names have been changed to protect the guilty.

DO THESE WORK BOOTS MAKE MY FEET LOOK FAT?

Kathleen McLaughlin

Mom's Prophecy

In 1948, my mom wrote a letter to her sister in Iowa. It appears as if my curiosity in vehicles was apparent even then:

"....Our baby is sure a rough and tough little individual. Today I rescued Kathy from the middle of the street, so from now on she has to stay locked up in the back yard whether she likes it or not. I keep telling her it's for her own good but that little scamp just won't listen. But we still think Kathy's a cute kid....She will be sixteen months old next week and plays with the neighbor boy and all she does is crawl around pushing little cars...."

The Boy's Vice Principal

Having a driver's license and a '52 Chevy inspired me to sign up for Auto Shop in my junior year at Point Loma High School, 1963. I proudly turned in my impending schedule for the upcoming fall semester consisting of, Russian, Art, Auto Shop and college prep courses.

About a week before the end of my sophomore year, I received a note asking me to report to the Boys' Vice Principal. *The Boys' Vice Principal? What for?* Shouldn't I have been summoned by the Girls' Vice Principal? I thought it was a mistake.

As I arrived at his office I showed the note to the secretary. She nonchalantly asked me to take a seat. I squirmed uneasily into the chair assuming I had been reported for parking in the "teacher's only" lot. Eventually he invited me into his office.

"Please have a seat…ah…Kathleen," he said looking at his notes to be certain he was talking to the right student.

I sat in the hard wooden chair, examining the office festooned with trophies won by previous boys' classes. He picked up a paper and read my proposed junior class schedule. He asked for reassurance. I confirmed those were the classes I had chosen.

"Now, Kathleen…or should I call you Kathy?"

"Either one is fine."

"Okay, Kathy it is," making a feeble pretense at being my buddy, "Now, Auto Shop is a class that fills up very fast."

4

I nodded and he beamed patronizingly. Then hesitantly, he asked why I thought I should take Auto Shop. I expounded on being the proud owner of a '52 Chevy and how I wanted to be able to work on it. I explained that my brother-in-law raced motorcycles and jalopies at Balboa Stadium and how I hoped to someday race myself.

He smiled condescendingly, "You know, Kathy, there are many boys who really *need* Auto Shop and I would like to ask you to take another course in consideration of the boys' future."

After some hesitation and removing the knife from my heart, I announced I would substitute another art course instead. He thanked me for my understanding and dismissed me in more ways than one. Tears made it difficult to see the combination on my locker. I grabbed the books I needed for homework that night and another door slammed shut.

In the future, I was determined to stick my foot in those doors and pry them open.

A Sign Of The Times

The sign on the counter at the employment office of San Diego Gas and Electric Company read: "Women applicants interested in manual labor, please inform the interviewer."

As a divorced mother of a six-year-old daughter, I was desperate. I had recently completed a course at a small private college to become a legal secretary. I had been searching for a position for several weeks and found nothing. Being a secretary was way down the list of my career choices as sitting at a desk all day did not appeal to me; but society and necessity had convinced me it was all I could do. It was July 1972.

My dad affectionately called me his "tomboy" since I preferred helping him sweep the garage over helping Mom sweep the kitchen. Boy-stuff just seemed a lot more fun. My original life plan was to go to college, get a degree, find a fun and lucrative career and maybe get married at twenty-five. By the time I was twenty-five, I had been married six years and divorced one. I had spent three of those years as an income tax consultant working for a small accounting firm, but taxes were seasonal and it was time for full-time employment.

The secretarial college sent me to some plush fancy law firms which paid minimum wage. Attorneys had left me cringing after divorcing Karen's dad, so I wasn't too keen on the idea of working for one of the slimy legal liars. I had applied at banks, thinking they might be interested in my tax

6

experience. They were impressed with my short resume, but had *"nothing available at this time."* SDG&E had an extensive legal department, so my intentions were to give corporate law a try with my limited legal secretary training.

"Excuse me," I said to the interviewer after reading the sign a second time, "just what does this mean? I mean the 'women applicants and the manual labor' part."

The scowl on his face revealed he was not enthused about having women working in non-traditional jobs. The interviewer sneered and grumbled, "If you can pick up a 90-pound jack-hammer and operate it you can have the job."

I scrutinized him. He was a short, scrawny stick-man and probably weighed all of 90-pounds himself. I thought, *"If he can do it, so can I."*

"I'm interested," I announced.

He grimaced. "Okay, fill this out," shoving a lengthy form in my direction.

I completed the form and was told *"nothing available at this time."* I proceeded to continue seeking employment elsewhere while persisting to pop in at the SDG&E employment office just to check, *"anything available?"*

Three months later – the phone rang. "Yes, I could come take a mechanical aptitude test. Yes, anytime. Yes, I would be there." I hung up, grabbed my dog, Lillian, and danced around my small living room. I slid to a stop, looked at Lillian and asked, "A *mechanical aptitude test? What the hell is that?"* She wagged her tail, indicating she didn't know either. The San Diego Public Library pulled me out of my mental quagmire. I took home several books with sample tests complete with answers. I studied diligently.

On test day, I was petrified. After stuffing a handful of nickels down the throat of a hungry parking meter, I arrived at the SDG&E employment office. Following signs taped to the wall with arrows and "Testing Room" handwritten on them, I found my destination and was confronted by the staff member conducting the test.

"Oh, you must be the girl," he remarked sardonically.

I smiled, nodded, and refrained from making comments about the obvious. He instructed me to sit anywhere and I looked for an empty seat. The only space available was a school-type desk in the middle of the room. Being the solitary woman encircled by twenty-three men was intimidating. Some sat smugly erect sporting white shirts and ties giving me the women-can't-do-anything-second-class-citizen look. Others slouched refusing to make eye contact. The staff member informed us that there were several positions in the company that required the passing of this particular test. Fortunately, I was not competing with all these men, but not knowing how many, the pressure was on. I needed to prove all those skeptical glaring eyes wrong. Dad taught me to fix a variety of things from broken chairs to washing machines. That experience and the library proved valuable. The exam was surprisingly effortless. The questions I had studied involved engineering calculations. The test I was given consisted of easy questions like one pulley vs. a system of pulleys - grade-school stuff - piece-acake – simple. I passed.

Within a few weeks, I received a call requesting a personal interview. I arrived twenty-minutes early. This time, an attractive thirty-something business-type woman dressed in medium heels, a sky-blue suit with a white starched blouse and stylish blond wavy hair was behind the employment counter. She greeted me with a welcoming smile and introduced herself. She intently examined my test results and résumé, frequently glancing up to study my face and confirming that I was, in fact, Kathleen. I assured her I was. She smiled again, excused herself and slipped over to the neighboring office of the Employment Manager. She stood in the door-way with her back to me. Straining, I could hear only fragments of the conversation.

"Look at her test scores," she said holding the piece of paper in front of him. The Manager glanced at it. He leaned over to peer around the woman and inspected me. He took a deep breath and frowned. I guessed my attire did not shout confidence. I was wearing a summer dress and sandals - I was a beach kid – a surfer - dark tan and bleached hair.

"Okay, send her in," he sighed, shaking his head with reluctance.

The woman motioned to me with a reassuring smile and nod. I entered and issued an appropriate salutation. The Manager, in his late-forties and balding, instructed me to sit down.

"You know you'll have to wear pants – jeans probably."

I acknowledged the fashion requirements. The Manager

did not often perform interviews personally, but in this case, he wanted to be certain he was making the right decision.

Did I know how to change a tire? *Yes*. Did I know how to use wrenches and screw-drivers? *Yes.* Had I ever performed any mechanical work? I explained that I raced motorcycles. I fudged a little and told him how I performed my own repairs. The reality was that I had only changed the spark plug – easy - and poured gas in the tank - real easy. But those qualified for repairs…sort of. Would I like a job working as a Helper in the Auto Repair Shop? The starting wage was $3.96 per hour. I nearly fainted. That was twice what the law offices had been offering, plus I wasn't going to have to buy a fancy new wardrobe. I thought it over for a nanosecond. *Yes, I would accept the position.* My exterior was composed and businesslike. My interior was turning cartwheels.

The next step was to meet with the Auto Repair Shop Supervisor. The Manager made a call and the appointment was immediate. I drove a few blocks to the facility located at Tenth and Imperial in the southeast portion of downtown San Diego. The huge repair garage, complete with mechanic pits covered with large work trucks and heavy construction equipment, was spread out over several urban acres. Behind every vehicle lingered a mechanic ready to size-up the new girl. The word had spread rapidly – within the hour. The security guard pointed me in the right direction. A weathered, thin man in his fifties sporting slacks, a white shirt and black tie, reminding me of a head waiter, stood waiting. He stood with his arms folded, examining me from top to bottom. Yes, my top. Yes, my bottom.

"I understand you want to work in the Auto Repair Shop."

"Yes, sir."

After a quick tour of the facility and explaining the duties of the Helper position, he asked, "Do you think you can handle the job? You'd be working nights."

The mechanics, leering from behind equipment and whispering to one another, were a little daunting, but, remembering the pay was sufficient for me and my daughter to live comfortably and independently, I managed another, "Yes, sir." Eyes rolled and heads shook in disgust.

"Okay, report Monday at 4:30 pm," he paused, "and be sure to wear pants."

Pants and Hair

When I was given the tour of the auto repair facilities by the ARS supervisor, I was told repeatedly that I would have to wear pants. The supervisor kept looking at the dress I chose to wear to the indoctrination. I regretted my fashion choice and continued to reassure him I understood the clothing requirements. It was obvious to me that jeans and work boots would be more appropriate to work in a garage than a sundress and sandals.

The pants issue was bigger than I realized. The 1970's was a time of change for women in the workplace. Pantsuits with a business-like jacket and matching slacks were becoming popular. But SDG&E had a dress code which restricted women from wearing anything but skirts and dresses.

The office women had been protesting the code for numerous fruitless years. More open-minded businesses had relaxed their fashion restrictions, but not SDG&E. Suddenly, there was a woman employee who was "required" to wear pants – me. As I arrived for my first day on the evening shift, dressed in jeans, work boots, a t-shirt and color-coordinating socks, I was greeted by several of the women workers as they were leaving for home. They smiled, made a quick assessment and wished me luck.

Within a few weeks, daring women in the offices began reporting for work in pantsuits. Some conservative supervisors complained, but the answer was always the same. "That woman in the garage wears pants, so I can too." Supervisors quit complaining. The dress code quietly vanished.

That first evening as I approached Number Two garage, the street was jam-packed with traffic. There were trucks double-parked, parked illegally and obstructing driveways. Number Two garage was immense; a full block long and a half a block wide with two large drive-through doors at either end. A large portion of the building was dedicated to tire repair. One bay was reserved for oil changing and several bays for repair work. It seemed more congested than when I had been given the personal tour by the supervisor the previous week.

As I entered the garage filled with the stench of automotive grease and oil, I heard whoops and hollers and turned to see what was causing the commotion. It was me. I was taken aback. I was stunned. I was embarrassed. Word had travelled like an electrical current throughout the company. Mechanics, helpers, laborers, and suits and ties had journeyed as many as twenty miles to see the "new girl helper." I should have charged admission.

As Brian, the tall burly redhead garage foreman struggled through the mob to meet me he screeched to a stop. Brian looked me over and seemed to approve of my attire. He paused and looked bamboozled. Something about me had him in a quandary. After we exchanged tense greetings, he invited me into his office. The crowd made derogatory remarks as to what Brian was going to do with me behind closed doors, ignoring the fact that the office had glass windows. He, not so kindly, told them to shut up and get back to work. I refrained from sticking my tongue out and saying, "neener, neener, neener." The sightseeing crowd began to disperse.

Once in Brian's office, I was offered a chair. I became anxious. I was wearing pants, work boots, a conservative t-shirt and even had a sweatshirt should the evening get chilly. What could be the problem?

My hair. That was the problem. It hung just past my shoulders in a straight hippy-surfer-style. The company had a policy that men could not have long hair, Brian explained. I was not a man, I pointed out. But, it seemed the rule was created for "safety" reasons for employees working in the garage and in construction. The concern was that a person with long hair could possibly get it caught in the engine fan belt, drive shafts, chain drives or under creepers. The dilemma was that the rule specifically said "men." The foreman didn't think he could instruct a woman to cut her hair. Now what?

After some discussion, I informed Brian that I'd take care of it. The following day I braided my hair, tied it on top of my head and sported a stocking cap. Problem solved… well sort of. Several of the men began to grow their hair long and wear stocking caps as well, much to the dismay of upper management.

I added "fashion trend-setter" to my resume.

Off the Wall

Being a frustrated interior designer/architect, the first week on the job I couldn't help but observed the structure of the building and the décor, or lack of. I noticed dark rectangles with faded outlines on the bulletin boards and the walls. It was apparent that posters or notices had been hanging, obviously for a long time, and possibly contained obsolete information. I was right about the posters, but mistaken about the content. A couple of weeks later pinups began to show some skin, but on another venue.

Each mechanic was required to buy their own toolbox and tools. The mechanics had massive carts with wheels and drawers called a roll-away. The roll-aways had the mechanics' names on them, locks and were considered personal property. This was the premise upon which the nudie-cuties began being displayed neatly hanging from the sides, back or front of the privately-owned toolboxes. I ignored the scantily clad photos ripped from the pages of "gentlemen's" magazines. This irritated some of the mechanics as it was apparent their whole purpose in life was to taunt me.

"Hey, come see my new tools," sneered a middle-aged, paunchy mechanic as he motioned with oil-stained hands.

"New tools?" I asked. I was cautious, but curious.

As I approached, he turned his roll-away around so I could see the newest addition to his poster collection.

"Like my new tools?" he smirked referencing the

15

extremely large breasts attached to a woman in a strategic position of which her mother would not approve.

"Oh, is this a photo of your wife?" I asked sardonically.

"No! That's not my wife."

"Oh, you just wish that was your wife."

"No," he frowned and waved his greasy hand, "get out of here."

I smiled and smugly sauntered away.

Burt Reynolds had recently made headlines with his questionable centerfold in the April 1972 issue of *Cosmopolitan* magazine. I was racing motorcycles at the time and subscribed to a couple of dirt-bike periodicals. Several of the motorcycle publications amusingly followed Burt's sexy lead, but their choice of skinny, or fat models, left something to be desired. I saw this as an opportunity to get a chuckle from my co-workers. Carefully, I removed the centerfold from my indiscriminate journals.

The following day, I arrived a few minutes early and sneaked my little poster from my lavender lunchbox. I scanned the area to see if I was under surveillance - all clear. Quickly I grabbed a couple of pushpins and placed my nudie not-so-cutie on the company bulletin board and escaped to my workstation. The bulletin board was located outside Brian, the night foreman's office. It was a gathering spot where the evening's repair orders were distributed. One by one the crowd assembled around my pinup.

"Who's that?" grumbled a tall awkward dude with no chin.

"Who put that up there?" questioned Mr. Beer-Belly.

"He's ugly," was the opinion of a scraggly guy with a yellow cigarette-stained mustache.

These were typical comments that dominated the conversation. It didn't take long to determine I was the one who posted the man-nude. They carefully examined the pinup. The motorcycle magazine, spoofing the Cosmopolitan and Burt, must have selected their centerfold by who drew the short straw. The druggy-looking dude they chose was thin, emaciated, hairy, bearded, sported long straggly hair and wore nothing but motorcycle boots. He lay in front of a chopper with a brassiere suggestively adorning the seat. A large bottle of inexpensive burgundy wine in his crotch gave the impression there was something significant to hide.

"Is this the type of guy you like?" inquired Brian.

"It's a joke," I explained to deaf ears.

"I think this is the type she likes," he glared and announced to his cohorts.

The comments cascaded into the gutter. I threw my hands up in surrender, shook my head in disgust, and retired to my work duties. The novelty dissipated as the mechanics and other co-workers became bored with picking apart my manly dandy. My joke had fallen flat on his naked butt. Within a few minutes the foreman handed me the pinup.

"We can't have nude, questionable or items of sexual content posted on company bulletin boards," he recited. "Here." He shoved the poster in my hand and continued, "They made us take all our stuff down the Friday before you showed up. The company was afraid you'd sue or something."

I learned the general consensus was that the company was not liable for what employees posted on their personal toolboxes. Brian stormed off.

"Well, that explains a lot," I said to thin air. Now I understood all the faded outlines on the bulletin boards and walls had at one time embraced pinup photos of scantily clad women. I, also, understood one more reason why they had all glared at me on my first day at work. Since I wasn't a mechanic, I didn't own a roll-away. I had nowhere to hang my nude dude, so back into the lunchbox he went.

VW Squeeze

After a particular wearisome evening, I was exhausted and ready to go home. I found my little forest-green 1957 Volkswagen with one mismatched fender snuggled between the bumpers of two intimidating vehicles. One was a four-wheel drive Dodge pickup with a lift-kit and a steel pipe front bumper inches away from my rear window and the other vehicle was a Chevy van, nestled close to the front of my little Bug. I waited nearly thirty-minutes for the culprits - devious employees - to make an appearance before I could go home. The "gentlemen" both worked in the Trouble Department located in the building across the street from the garage. The Trouble Department, a 24/7 sector, received calls from customers concerning power outages or natural gas leaks and dispatched repairmen to the job. As the two approached their vehicles with apologetic words regurgitating from their raspy throats, I smiled sweetly and realized I would have to pay the baby-sitter overtime.

Innocently, my first impression was that the parking issue was a mistake, an error, maybe poor driving on their part. Not being used to this type of conduct, it took a few days before I realized it was the same two vehicles and obviously an exhibit of contempt. At that point it became a personal challenge. I started parking a block or two away or close to a driveway, street corner, or fire hydrant. Soon my adversaries gave up.

I had won this round, by default.

19

Set Up

When I interviewed for the position of mechanic's helper I was asked if I knew how to change a tire. I had answered yes.

As a teenager learning to drive, my father was fearful that I should be stranded in the boonies with a flat tire. He taught me how to use the car-jack, remove the flat and replace it with the spare. At SDG&E, changing a tire meant something entirely different. The tires they were referring to were over three feet tall and mounted on three-piece rims. I had no inkling how to repair one of those rubber monsters.

Training for new helpers consisted of following an "experienced" employee around. My mentor had been on the job for all of three weeks. His name was Rick, nineteen years old – six years my junior - energetic and sympathetic to my situation. He was only a couple of inches taller than me, average build and eagerly attempting to grow a mustache. Rick was a good instructor and took some ribbing for being stuck with the new "girl helper." He spent the first week showing me around the eight-block facility, explaining what activities took place in each area, showing me where tools were and how to use them, if he knew, and introducing me to other employees.

After a couple of months of running errands, delivering parts from one garage to another and additional uncomplicated duties, I was ready to be trained on tire repair. I discovered this alteration in routine upon my arrival at work on that fateful day early in 1973. There was no previous warning. I entered the garage, lavender lunchbox in hand, noticing a small crowd beginning to assemble in a manner reminiscent of my first day. I assumed a meeting was about to take place or someone was retiring and everyone was gathering to offer best wishes. I received the usual, *"hi-how-are-ya,"* smiles, glares and occasional mention, *"so, this is your big day."*

"What big day?" I asked. No response - just raised eyebrows and smirks.

Rick greeted me with a somber expression. "You're gonna learn to change tires."

He pointed me in the direction of the tire repair area. Juan, my new mentor, had been on tire duty two weeks. He was in his early twenties, over six-feet tall, wore a blue and gold San Diego Charger's t-shirt, and had no problem moving excessively large tires and immense steel rims.

Normally, Juan was friendly and usually offered a smiling salutation. This evening he was quiet and aloof. I inquired if everything was okay. Juan ignored my question and began his instructions. He explained briefly the use of the tools which were all stacked next to the wall or hanging from hooks near the tire cage. The tire cage was an ominous looking structure of steel pipe about four-feet high, three-feet deep and five-feet wide. Juan explained that after a tire was repaired and placed back on the rim, it was put into the cage to inflate. The cage was for safety reasons. If the rim was not put together correctly, it could explode while being inflated.

Explode! The cage showed evidence of previous tire casualties.

With the crowd intently watching, Juan instructed me to follow his every move. One truck tire was ready to be repaired. He showed me how to remove the valve stem from the tire to let any remaining air out. I obeyed. Juan handed me a crowbar and told me how to remove the outside ring from the rim. I obeyed. Juan showed me how to test the tube for leaks. I obeyed. With every step, Juan was exceptionally thorough in his instruction. We removed the tube, installed a new one, reassembled the rim, placed the tire in the cage and aired it up. It did not explode. The crowd lingered.

"Now you get to do one on your own," Juan told me.

He brought another flat to the repair area. Handed me the tools and walked away.

"Where are you going?" I asked in desperation. One walk-through was not enough. I wanted help at least one more time to learn these new skills.

"I was told you had to do this one on your own," Juan said gravely.

"Could you just watch me to see if I do it right?"

Juan shook his head. The audience gradually became larger. Men from the neighboring facilities came to watch the evening's entertainment. Some I recognized, some I did not. Some were in greasy coveralls with stained coffee cups in hand; some were in three-piece suits sporting red power-ties. All were watching me. I was uneasy, nervous, petrified.

As I studied the lifeless tire lying at my feet trying to

remember step one, I heard a sound over my left shoulder. It was Juan with another dead tire.

"What is everyone here for?" I whispered to Juan.

"To watch you fail."

"What?" I was astonished, shaken, embarrassed and angered.

Juan shushed me, winked and smiled. He was a man I could trust.

"Do what I do," he whispered.

Juan began repairing his tire. He moved with slow deliberate motions allowing me to mimic. I glanced sideways when I was unsure of my next step. One of the members of our "fan club" criticized Juan for moving too slow. Juan ignored the remark.

When both tires were complete, Juan asked me to air his tire first. I placed it in the cage and began to apply air through the valve. As I did, I noticed Juan casually inspecting my repair job. When his tire was full of air - with no explosion - he smiled as he placed my tire in the cage – again, no explosion. As we finished airing the tires, I became aware of our audience gradually dissipating. A disgruntled mechanic was heard to comment, "Damn, I guess she's here to stay." One of the suits moaned, "No excitement, guess I'll go home."

Juan gestured for me to follow him as he walked outside the garage. As soon as we were away from criticizing ears, he revealed his instructions. He was fuming. The foreman had told him to show me once and once only. If I could not change a tire by myself after one lesson, then I would be "let go" and it was rumored, the company would not have to hire any more women as mechanics' helpers. Juan informed me that all the male helpers were given several days, even weeks, to learn.

"Unfair," he grumbled.

Fruits and Nuts

The night shift and the day shift overlapped. This was an attempt at communication between the vehicle operators working the day shift and the mechanics working nights. It was during the overlap I was approached by Mr. Jenkins, a stern old guy with droopy eyelids and a cleft chin who always wore an Aussie outback hat. I was in my fourth week of tire repair and getting the hang of it. Mr. Jenkins sternly demanded his tires be exchanged for some with a different tread. He claimed the vehicle rode too rough.

"What do you do for the company?" I inquired in my most girlie voice. I had determined that I received better response when I was thought to be "cute." Jenkins relaxed a bit. His voice softened.

"I inspect the transmission roads," he responded. He continued to explain how he examined the dirt roads paralleling the electric transmission lines and reported any necessary repairs. The roads had to be in prime condition so the crews could reach problem areas in an emergency.

The tires on his 1970 Ford Bronco were appropriate for his job. I knew from my own off-road experience that those tires rode a little rough on pavement, but that was the price one had to pay for traction in the dirt. I shrugged, obliged and replaced the tires with some to his liking.

The following week Jenkins returned. "These tires are not working. Could you put the other tires back on?"

Mr. Jenkins scrutinized every step in the process. He

would frown, smile, then grumble inaudibly and saunter away. My experience in dune-buggies and off-roading caused me to mentally analyze the situation. I mentioned it to Brian and suggested something else might be the problem with the vehicle. Brian grumbled, reluctant to take advice from a girl, and said he'd have a mechanic look into it.

The chosen mechanic, Aaron, a forward-thinking individual, discussed the history of the problem with me and took the situation seriously. After taking the vehicle for a test drive and crawling underneath to examine a few things, he concluded the shock absorbers needed to be replaced. Aaron replaced them and left a note for Jenkins.

The following evening as I reported to work, Mr. Jenkins was waiting for me with a paper bag and his usual scowl.

"I wonder what the problem is now," I mumbled to myself and greeted him with a sugary smile.

"Here," he said sternly offering me the bag.

"What's this?" I inquired as I cautiously accepted the bag and gingerly peeked inside.

"Some peaches off the neighbor's tree and tomatoes from my garden."

"Off the neighbor's tree?"

"We share," he responded with a slight grin.

I thanked Mr. Jenkins and he mumbled something about being sorry for causing me extra work with the tire changing. I lied and told him it was not a problem. Jenkins provided me with fresh fruits and vegetables for several years until he retired.

Never Give Flowers

I avoided spending the 9:00 PM lunch break with the night mechanics for two reasons: 1) I didn't care much for their company; 2) I thought I should give them some man-space.

I began eating in a small break room in the building across the street from the garage. Occasionally, I was joined by Bill, the night janitor, a small, gentle, soft-spoken man in his early sixties. It wasn't long before Bill and I cultivated a friendship. He didn't own a car and had an aversion to flying so he had traveled the entire country by bus or train. His experiences were fascinating and I listened to his stories until past our break time. The building also housed the only available women's restroom, so, many times, I used that as my excuse for being late getting back to work.

Bill and I also shared a passion for the legitimate theatre. I had become interested as a youngster when I was dragged to my sister's rehearsals. He would tell me about theatres and performances he attended in New York, Los Angeles, Salt Lake City and San Diego's Old Globe Theatre. Bill was an intellectual man who loved life. Before he retired in April, 1976, he gave me a special book. It had been given to him by his father for Christmas 1934: *The Complete Works of Shakespeare.* The following weekend, when curled up on my couch, thumbing through the Bard's work, I discovered newspaper clippings tucked neatly inside. They were from a 1933 New York Times Mid-Week Pictorial featuring E. H.

27

Sothern; a 1947 Salt Lake Tribune article highlighting Roddy McDowell and Orson Wells: and a more current 1974 San Diego Union piece presenting Laurence Olivier. The next Monday evening I sought after Bill and asked if he wanted the clippings back. He laughed and confessed he had forgotten about them. The clippings were from a few of the many performances he had attended staring his favorite actors. He said, "No, you will appreciate them more than any of my relatives. You keep them."

One of the most moving stories Bill relayed took place when he was four-years-old. A kindly neighbor woman frequently gave him and his sister sugar cookies cut in animal shapes in the summer and snowmen and bells at Christmas. One spring day, as he passed a bed full of gorgeous flowers, he stopped to admire the floral display. Bill decided to pick a flower as a gift to the woman. The bed was bursting with daffodils, roses and daisies. He selected a small lovely flower feeling it was perfect for his friend. He knocked on her back door and proudly offered the yellow blossom. She smiled sweetly and thanked him. As Bill was leaving her porch, he glanced over his shoulder. Just before she closed the door, he saw her toss the flower in the trash. Bill discovered years later that the flower had been a dandelion, but to a four-year-old a flower is a flower even if it is a weed. He was sixty-one when he told me this story. Bill never gave any woman flowers again.

I still have Bill's book.

Too Darn Nice

The company transferred employees to various locations usually asking for volunteers. In the late spring of 1974, I took advantage of an opening at Rose Canyon, one of the satellite districts. It was closer to home and - weather permitting - I could ride my bicycle to work. The district employees thought of themselves as a family. But, like most families, there exists a member everyone tries to avoid. I, unwittingly, became that person.

I tried to be friendly and sociable, but to no avail. I repeatedly asked myself what the problem was. I was agreeable, well-mannered, inquisitive – *what could it be?* After a couple of weeks of "solitary confinement" I asked Ernie, the garage foreman, why everyone was avoiding me.

"You're too nice," he said matter-of-factly, curling the ends of his salt and pepper handlebar mustache.

"Too nice?" I asked aghast. I had been accused of a lot of things in my life, but being *too nice* was *not* one of them.

"Yep," he affirmed, "the guys are afraid they might offend you if they swear or say the wrong thing."

"I'll be damned," I puzzled. "Could you please tell them they can relax? It's not as if I haven't heard cuss words before and most of them I've used myself at some time or other."

He smiled, revealing a missing front tooth. "I'll tell 'um."

Ernie kept his word. Gradually the mechanics nodded greetings and struck up idle conversations. I knew I was finally being accepted when I was invited to stay for the "music-fest." The night shift was over at 1:00 AM. It was useless to hit the bars after work since they all closed at 2:00 and final drink orders were usually taken at 1:30. On Friday nights, after closing the office and putting the tools away, the work benches were re-purposed to support musicians playing banjos, guitars, harmonicas and keyboards. One of the mechanic's would disappear and return with a couple of six-packs of beer. The night crew at Rose Canyon had various degrees of talent; some good, some mediocre. Since my daughter spent Friday nights with her grandparents, I had time to party. I had been playing guitar for several years and even performed at *"The End,"* a small coffee shop in Pacific Beach. My strings and singing talents fit right in. The music was great – well…maybe not - but we all had fun. It became a weekly event until upper management found out and squelched it. We all had suspicions as to who might have ratted on us. The general consensus was that it was one of two grumpy fleet supervisors, or maybe both. A memo was distributed putting a stop to any "after hour events" on company property.

Tasting Dirt

Perhaps it was because I was eleven, excited and I was actually going out after dark, but it seemed like a long twenty-mile drive from Ocean Beach to El Cajon. My oldest sister, Kay, had married Norman, a motorcycle fanatic. Norman was going to race his motorcycle in a dirt-track event at Cajon Speedway. It was 1958. We arrived to air filled with dust and exhaust, the smell of gasoline and oil, the constant shouting of the announcer and the cheering of the crowd. After buying tickets, we picked up some popcorn and found uncomfortable seats in the metal grandstands. Kay and her friends, with their coiffures styled in big bouffant of beehives and flips, were screaming with excitement as the bikes scooted past, smacked into the guard fence or crashed into each other. The thumping sound of the four-stroke engines made my little kid heart stop. The noise. The speed. The thrill. As it's been said, "Four wheels move the body. Two wheels move the soul." I loved it.

Only a Biker Knows Why a Dog Sticks His Head Out Of a Car Window

I love the desert, but only between October and April when the weather is tolerable. That was motorcycle desert racing season.

My brother-in-law, Norman, is to blame for getting me all enthralled with the two-wheeled machines. Norman's first encounter with desert racing was in 1959 and the legendary 150-mile "Big Bear Hare and Hound" northeast of Los Angeles. Norman loved adventure. He began racing in our local desert east of San Diego in 1960. Over the next ten years, Mom, Dad and I ventured out several times to watch the excitement. But it wasn't until 1970 that I felt the tug on my bra strap to join the dusty, thrilling, grimy, exhilarating, filthy, stimulating, sweaty - sometimes freezing - sport.

Norman and Kay had invited me to join them for the weekend. My nephew, Bob, and niece, Pam, both teenagers, had already been racing for a couple of years. Pam was racing "Powder Puff" with about eight other women ranging in age from sixteen to forty. I watched with envy. Bravely loaning me their bikes, and eventually, my new friends and relatives taught me how to ride. I gradually sneaked aside some grocery money and eventually bought my first dirt bike, a yellow Yamaha. I painted an image of the Chiquita Banana logo on the tank.

Morris, a tall, lanky young man who had been riding since he could walk, took me and a couple of other novices for an educational ride.

"Follow me," he said "and do what I do when I do it. If I stand up, you stand up. If I give it gas, you give it gas."

Morris was amazing and I followed his instructions impeccably or, at least, tried. He built confidence in me and the other novices, teaching us to ride through rough and rocky trails and how to speed through sandy washes.

Morris's motto: "Look where you want to go, not where you don't want to go."

That became my maxim for life. I have followed Morris' teaching (most of the time) to the present day.

My Chiquita Banana Yamaha was more of a trail bike than a race bike. It was street legal and didn't have the suspension required to carry me over the rocks and ravines in the desert. After a year or so, I sold it and purchased a 125cc Bultaco. The Bultaco was a magnificent race bike...for someone else. The bike was described by the more experienced as being "pipie." That meant that I could give it throttle and it would lug along for a few seconds, then suddenly the power would hit. The bike would take off, pulling a wheelie. If I wasn't hanging on tight...off the back I went. It was nerve-wracking.

I rode my 1972 Bultaco in the Lake Elsinore Grand Prix in Riverside County north of San Diego. Hundreds of entries filled the streets of the small California town. I waited two hours before my line moved to the official "start." The race was exhausting as I tried to conquer the rough terrain on a motorcycle that had an evil mind of its own. But hearing the crowd and especially the women cheering me on instilled the courage I needed to complete the race. I didn't win the women's division; I seldom won anything, but I couldn't let my "fans" down. I finished.

I sold the Bultaco and bought a 125cc DKW, a motorcycle manufactured by the German motorcycle and automobile maker, Dampf-Kraft-Wagen. They had been around since 1916. The DKW initials for the motorcycle became *Das Kleine Wunder*—"the little marvel". I affectionately nicknamed my bike Deek and it proved to be my best buddy. It had a springer front suspension which made it a little heavy, but dependable. Deek and I raced many motocross and desert races, took trips to Mexico and had good times and bad.

The Adventures of Deek

Peering through blood-shot eyes, I could see the dust of a vehicle approaching over the Mexican horizon. The distinctive sound of a Volkswagen Baja Bug became louder as it clunked and bumped over the gashes and ruts in the dirt road. This was my first sign of human life in over half an hour. Rush-hour traffic was definitely not a concern on this isolated high-desert clay road in the middle of Baja California. It was May 1974, and hot. I struggled to my feet, helmet in hand, and began waving frantically at the approaching dust cloud.

"What the hell am I doing here," I mumbled.

As the dust cloud became larger I could faintly see a bright yellow Baja Bug. I was praying it was accompanied by a pickup truck – a truck with an empty bed or at least room enough to haul me and my broken motorcycle to the next dinky Mexican town, but no. The Bug was traveling at racing speed. I was sure they were here for the same reason I was – to pre-run the Baja 500 Off-Road Race.

The Baja 500 is one of the oldest and most prestigious off-road races in existence. Everyone who was anyone was in Baja on this Memorial Day weekend to test the 500-kilometer course, even if they had no intention of competing in the race itself. *What was an old-enough-to-know-better woman doing by herself stranded in Baja with a broken motorcycle?* Adventure! I loved adventure. But this was not what I had in mind.

35

The events leading up to this moment fogged my mind like some wicked nightmare. I had gone to Ensenada, Baja California, Mexico to meet some friends. We were going to pre-run the course on our motorcycles. I had been racing motorcycles in the Southern California deserts for several years and was looking forward to the challenge. To see the Baja 500 course first hand was a dirt-bike rider's dream. I had been looking forward to this trip for weeks.

Upon arrival at the designated meeting spot – a vacant lot across the street from the El-something-or-other restaurant – I was informed by the other members of the group that my friend would not be joining us. Seemed she had to work. Since I had never met any of her friends in this group, she had given them a description of my vehicle – a little lemon-yellow '72 Chevy LUV truck with small flowers painted just behind the side windows – very cute. She also described my 125cc DKW motorcycle, which I affectionately called Deek. They spotted me immediately.

I was hesitant to join a group consisting entirely of men I didn't know. I should have gone with those instincts. A couple of them I knew by reputation. They were some of the fastest dirt bike racers in Southern California. The racers, Tom, Scott and Jim, were younger than me by at least five years. They appeared to be clones of one another. Dressed in full racing leathers and boots, the only disparity was the color of their leathers. Tom's uniform-of-the-day was white with red and a gold stripe on the side. At least I think that was Tom. Scott was beige with a blue stripe - I think. And

Jim's attire consisted of leather pants and a long-sleeved jersey with *Husqvarna* across the front.

The other gentlemen were much older. Mr. Beyer, a hunched over middle-aged rugged man, was the father of Tom and Scott. His t-shirt had seen better days. The collar was tattered and the front was stained by many sloppy hamburgers and dropped ketchup-drenched fries. His jeans had been used as a grease-rag for motorcycle repairs. The other older man, Silent Man, never spoke and I was never introduced. He stared through blood-shot eyes and smirked with tarnished teeth at me every time he caught my eye. He wore a t-shirt draped like a small tent over his anemic frame. His cowboy boots and jeans were dusty.

They seemed harmless enough and I had seen them at the local desert races many times. Tom and Scott were planning on actually competing in the "Big Race" about four weeks away. They had their racing bikes and planned on covering the course at race speeds. Jim was just along for the ride. Mr. Beyer was to follow in a grimy Ford van pockmarked by previous off-road pre-runs. The van carried the supplies, tools, spare parts for the race bikes and camping gear. Silent Man would ride with Mr. Beyer.

They were all justifiably serious about the upcoming race. It could be profitable for the winner, not only in prize money, but in product endorsements. I was concerned I might slow them down. Not to worry, I was told. I could definitely tag along. They knew my reputation as a desert racer and assured me I would be able to keep up. I was flattered. Besides, the van would be following at a slower pace. Sounded safe enough to me.

The plan was to leave my truck and Jim's truck in the vacant lot in Ensenada near the starting point of the race. We would then travel on our bikes to the halfway point today - Saturday. This would be somewhere near Bahia de Los Angeles, or commonly known to us gringos, as LA Bay, on the Gulf of California. Then, on Sunday, we would travel to the finish point back in Ensenada.

I loaded up my backpack with the essentials –a light jacket, a change of clothes and a personal hygiene satchel. I tied my sleeping bag on the back fender of Deek. Assured that they had enough food, I still grabbed a can of tuna and some crackers – just in case. A large canteen of water was attached to the handlebars of my bike and one on my belt. I didn't have a map of the course as my friend – the no-show – was to furnish it. I wiped the sweat from my forehead with my bandana, tucked it in my front pocket and put on my helmet – the one with the flowers painted on the side. With my wallet stuffed in my back pocket, I locked up my little yellow truck. I was ready.

I had flooded the carburetor in my zest to get on with this journey, but the others took off without waiting to see if I got going or not. This should have been my first clue that these were not compassionate people. They were unquestionably from the "me-first" generation. Finally, I got Deek started, poured on the gas and took off into the middle of traffic without looking. I was in a hurry to catch up with the rest of the group. Cars honked and people yelled what sounded like obscenities in Spanish and waved a universally known middle finger. All this appeared to be directed at me. I swerved to avoid a truck, regained my composure and decided that a more reasonable speed and attentiveness were in order.

The first part of the course paralleled the paved highway, which was only a two-lane road, but well defined. After about 15 miles I came across a checkpoint. The Mexican officials were checking visas. Unfortunately, I didn't have one. I pulled a "Lucy Ricardo" and told them that my "esposo" had my visa and had gone through several minutes before. In my limited Spanish and a lot of hand gestures, I described the van and the officials nodded in acknowledgement that they had remembered seeing it. But, they still wanted my visa. I explained again, but this time I managed to squeeze out some tears. They felt sorry for me and let me pass.

After about two and a half hours, I caught up with the rest of the group in the shade of a small lonely oak tree. They were just finishing up a snack and beer stop, clue number two. A beer stop was not on my agenda, as I like to be clear-headed when riding my motorcycle.

"Where've ya been?" was the only question asked. I was about to tell them, but they were packing up to hit the road. I asked about a snack and was told it had been stored away. I would have to wait until lunch, only a few more hours. Okay, I could wait. I wasn't that hungry – not really. Off they went. I was going to grab a cracker from my backpack, but decided that since I still didn't have a map of the course, I should stick close to the group.

This time I kept up. Following the van meant being engulfed in dust. The powder-fine grime managed to sneak in the small vents on the side of my goggles. My eyes burned. After a few miles of this, I decided to slow up just enough to keep the van in sight, but far enough back to stay clear of most of the filthy wake. I was cruising along at a comfortable speed. Then, like a roadside bomb, a race car tore past spraying me with gravel. I wore leather gloves and racing vest, jeans, a long-sleeved shirt, lineman boots and kneepads. But the small rocks managed to hit my cheeks and neck, the only parts not covered. *Ouch!* I slowed and moved over to the right side of the road. I wanted to give those racers plenty of room. Another car sped by, then another and another. By the time the dust had settled, the van had disappeared.

I increased my speed to catch up, but came upon one of those villainous forks-in-the-roads. *Which way should I go?*

Both directions seemed to be equally traveled. I waited a few minutes hoping for another racer to come by. Hooray! A race truck sped toward me. I wisely decided to putsy on over to the side of the road out of harm's way. The truck took the right fork. Following was a smaller pickup with the bed full of gas cans and toolboxes. The driver saw me and came sliding to a stop.

"You okay?" the passenger asked.

"I'm fine. Just didn't know which way the course went from here."

The passenger mumbled something to the driver and reached into his glove compartment.

"Here's a map. We've got plenty." Off they went before I could say, "bless you my child."

I felt solace in this piece of paper. I carefully folded the map and tucked it in my pocket. I didn't look at it. After all, the guys that gave it to me had plenty of maps. They must know where they were going. I followed my saviors' tracks.

Lunchtime came and went and my companions were nowhere to be seen. I cruised along passing other pre-runners having lunch breaks, fixing blown tires or just taking a rest. Other pre-runners passed me like I was going backwards. I pushed on. I had filled up my gas tank at a small town several hours before. A quick visual inspection revealed about half a tank. The van was supposed to be carrying spare gas. Since the sun was heading toward the summer solstice the days were long. I wiped the dirt from the face of my watch. It was 7 PM.

About eighty miles east of our starting point, I approached a small valley with an abundance of native oak trees for shade from the late-day sun. The valley was inundated with improvised campsites. About 40 or 50 fellow pre-runners had settled in for the night. I circled the motley groups, slowing so as not to stir up too much dust. I am a polite rider. The familiar van was spotted parked with the doors open, tools spread out all over the ground and one of the motorcycles with its internal guts lying lifeless on a raggedy tarp.

"Hi" I said.

Silent Man just nodded. Mr. Beyer mumbled something about Scott's motorcycle having some mechanical problems. At least, I think that is what he said. His comments were all jumbled up with profanities.

"There's some sandwich stuff in the ice chest if you want something to eat." Tom said as he gestured with an oily hand in the direction of the cooler. "I hope there's something left."

"Thanks." I headed for the cooler. I was starving. All I had consumed was a couple of swigs of water from my canteen. I opened the cooler and found a slice of bread and a soggy piece of cheese spotted with greasy fingerprints floating in the melted ice. I ate both. I had considered scarfing down my tuna and crackers, but from the looks of things I determined I would be better off hanging on to those rations awhile longer. The rest of the cooler was filled with beer.

After finishing the beer and my paltry meal, I began looking for the ladies room, better known as a "private" bush. There were plenty of bushes, but they all seemed to be occupied by campers. I walked down the road and as I was leaving the camp I recognized my map-givers. They recognized me, too.

"Hey! Sorry about the wrong turn. I guess we were supposed to take the left fork in the road. I think it would have cut off about 10 miles," the passenger shouted. "Hope you didn't follow us."

"I did," I said smiling with my bottom teeth, "it's okay." I continued my search for a private bush. I found one.

Returning to the camp, I discovered everyone sulking. The broken motorcycle seemed to be terminal. It had received a mechanical fatal blow. There was talk of returning to Ensenada and not finishing the course. We decided to sleep on it and spread our sleeping bags out on the ground. I carefully checked for snakes and scorpions before settling in. The theory was that the ailing motorcycle might heal itself overnight.

Sunrise arrived way too early and was met by the sound of motorcycle and racecar engines. I crept from my sleeping bag to find part of the group already packed and ready to go home. The new plan was that Mr. Beyer, Silent man and Scott were going back to Ensenada with Scott's broken bike. Tom and Jim were going to continue on course. They had left Jim's pickup truck in Ensenada with mine so there would not be a problem getting home. I had my choice of following the van or the racers. Since I had not made any wise choices so far, I decided not to break my record. I continued on with the racers. The van was packed and the other three were homeward bound in minutes. I was not too worried about food, as I knew there was a cantina at LA Bay. For breakfast I munched on tuna, crackers and cold coffee.

Since I was slower than the racers, I decided to hit-the-road first and get a head start. Reviewing the map with Tom and Jim, I felt confident that *this* time I knew where I was going. I climbed on Deek and kicked the starter…nothing. I kicked again…nothing. At that moment, I hated Deek. I began searching through my backpack for my little tool kit and an extra sparkplug. Tom, a know-it-all-kinda-guy came to my "rescue." He whipped out his sparkplug wrench from his pocket and grabbed a plug from his tool kit.

"I have extras," he announced confidently and began valiantly working on my disagreeable motorcycle.

I studied the map again while he changed the plug for me. I had forgotten one little tiny minor thing. My DKW required a short reach plug - a spark plug with a shorter end on it than regular sparkplugs. Not working on my own bike would become a major faux pas.

With my bike again in running order, off I went. I followed some other pre-runners who seemed to be just there for the fun as they were not traveling at racing speed. I surmised that if I were ahead of Tom and Jim maybe I wouldn't get left behind - a reasonable assumption.

About two hours into the second day's trip, my rather trusty motorbike began to emit an unusual noise. I kept on riding. The noise was not going away. I began to worry – not that I had anything to worry about. After all, I was a couple of hundred miles from home in the high-desert of Baja California, traveling with people I did not know, on a motorcycle making funny noises. Deek let me down. It came to a slow stop.

I climbed off and took a sip of water. I was grateful I still had some left. I stared at the disabled bike, as if staring would cause it to repair itself. I made an attempt to start it. *Nothing.* I made another attempt. *Still nothing.* I decided to check the gas. *Yep, had some.* I checked the chain. *Yep, it was still there and still tight.* Now I inspected the sparkplug knowing it had been changed a couple of hours before and should still be good. I took my plug-wrench from my tool kit and removed the plug. I examined it carefully as if I knew what I was doing. *Hummmm.* Even I could tell something was strange. The plug was covered with tiny bits of metal. *Hummmm.* After carefully checking for any stray reptiles, I sat down in the dirt to ponder the situation.

I must have stared at that plug for more than fifteen minutes. My mind kept wandering to thoughts of why the hell I was in Mexico when I could have spent the weekend at the beach sipping wine coolers. I searched my tool kit for another spark plug. I found one in the bottom of the bag carefully wrapped in its original box. I removed it from its safe, clean environment and screwed it into place.

"Okay," I mumbled. "Start damn you."

I jumped on the kick-starter. *Nothing.* Jumped again. *Nothing.* I began a kick-starting frenzy jumping on the starter over and over until I was exhausted. *Nothing.* It has been my experience, before and since, that mechanical devices need a person knowledgeable in mechanics to repair them. That person is not, was not, and never will be, me.

I climbed from Deek and sank to the ground. I cried. The tears were fifty percent frustration and fifty percent exhaustion. It was hot. I was tired. Removing my gloves, I pulled my helmet from my sweaty head. I wiped my dirty sticky forehead with my bandana. A motorcycle helmet totally destroys any coiffure. My imperfect doo was a mess. I ran my fingers through my damp hair. I stared down at Deek. A weak gnawing sound reminded me of my hunger. The tuna, crackers and cold coffee indulged a few hours before had not sustained me. While in this semi-conscious state, I heard the high-pitched whine of a typical two-stroke race bike engine. To the untrained ear it's obnoxious, but to me it was the sound of human life – well, sort of. It was Tom and Jim. I waved them down. Amazingly, they stopped.

"Anything wrong?" asked Jim.

"Yes, but I am not sure what." As they got off their bikes and squatted next to Deek, I continued, "I took the sparkplug out and there are little bits of metal on the end. What do you suppose could cause that?"

Tom grabbed the metal-flaked plug from my hand and examined it.

"Gee, I don't know," he said with a curious tone and handed the defective plug to Jim. He just grunted and handed it back to me.

"Have you tried a new plug?" inquired Tom.

"Yep," I said with a large amount of honest discouragement in my voice.

"Wonder what's wrong?" Jim grunted.

We all stared at Deek.

"Let me try it," Tom commanded as he ordered me aside with a wave of his hand like the King of Racedom. Eagerly I obeyed, hoping that Deek merely needed the masculine touch. Nothing. I must admit that the feminist in me was relieved to know that it wasn't just me and that Deek was, in fact, broken. Then a reality check reminded me of where I was and what was happening, or not happening. *Deek was broken!*

"Well," Tom said as he swung his leg over his motorcycle, "Hope you get it fixed."

My eyes opened about as wide as my mouth gaped. They were going to leave me here – miles from civilization.

"We'll tell someone where you are," offered Jim. I was too surprised to even imagine that they were going to abandon me. I could not utter a sound. All I could do was watch in shock as they rode off. Again, I cried. Then the mumbling started. I began to carry on a conversation with myself.

Who were they going to tell? They didn't really know me or how to get in touch with my family. How was I going to get back to my truck, much less get home? Who the hell did they think they were leaving me out here like this? I would not have left them.

I hated life.

Then I heard the sound of something with an enormously large engine coming my way. Like a slap in my dirty face, I realized that I was not the only one on this road. There were hundreds of pre-runners out on the course this weekend. Someone was sure to save this damsel in distress. The image of a race truck was approaching at full speed. *Hooray! I was saved.* It sped past me. *Were they blind? Why didn't they stop?* I kicked a nearby plant. I kicked it again. Regaining my composure, I decided to quit taking my frustrations out on the flora and fauna. I sat down. For nearly half an hour I drew arrows in the dirt with my boot. I pulled out a small notebook from my pack and began writing my last will and testament: *"I, Kathleen Ann, leave everything I own, including the $187.32 in my savings account, to my daughter, Karen Ann and our little dog, Lillian..."*

I stood up. I paced. I sat. I stood up again. I sat again. It was while in this state of uncertainty and annoyance that I heard another vehicle approaching. I jumped up. This time I stood in the middle of the road and waved my arms. They would either have to stop- hopefully, run off the road to pass me - maybe, or run me down - hopefully not.

Success! The vehicle stopped. It was another Baja Bug, too small to consider giving me a ride not to mention ol' Deek. The driver, a thirty-something bearded stick-man and his navigator, a twenty-something fat guy were nice and seemed genuinely concerned, which was definitely more than I could say about my traveling companions – or ex-traveling companions.

I explained my predicament. The men looked at one another, then at Deek, then at me, and then at one another. They pulled to the side of the road and the driver hopped out. His navigator struggled to remove his over-sized body from the undersized vehicle. They took off their helmets and attempted to shake off the dirt and grunge.

"Hooray," I thought, *"Help at last!"*

They asked the usual questions. Have you checked the gas? *Yes, I had plenty.* Have you checked the plug? *Yes. I produced the offending plug from my pocket.* They examined it. One of the men asked to see one of the plugs I had carried as a spare. He held them up side by side. The dissimilarity was obvious. The plug Tom had placed in Deek's cylinder head was too long. It had punched a hole in the piston.

"Oh, no!" I gasped. Realizing the problem, I struggled to keep more tears from further clouding my vision. I hate it when I do that "girl-stuff," but I was devastated. I should never have let Tom replace the sparkplug. I should have done it myself. My only defense was that it never occurred to me that a "top star" racer wouldn't realize that not all motorcycles use the same type of plugs. The two men were about to utter the usual grunts and snorts accompanying perplexing thought, when a strange sound came over the horizon. We looked in the direction of the oncoming vehicles. They were not quite moving at race speeds, but still at an extremely fast clip.

As the first vehicle became visible, I squinted and remarked, "What is that?"

The Baja Bug driver answered, "It's a Citron Mahari. The other car's a Saab. We passed them a few miles back."

The Citron and the Saab pulled up to a stop just past the Baja Bug. I had not seen this many vehicles in one spot since camp the night before. The Citron driver and his navigator stepped out and removed their helmets. The Saab crew pulled off to the side of the road a little further up and joined the group. All were 1970-type nerds in their mid-twenties. They appeared as if they would have been more at ease behind an accounting desk or in a physics lab, looking dreadfully like clones fully clad in dusty sport shirts and slacks - not exactly the off-road-racing type.

Then a strange phenomenon occurred. It was suddenly as if I did not exist. The men in the Baja Bug began talking to the men in the Saab and the Citron about what they were all going to do with Deek and me. I thought to myself, *"Helloooo! Here I am. Don't I have a say in this?"* My feminist side was attempting escape, but I managed to arrest it just in time. Realizing that these men were discussing a way to get me out of this predicament, I, for once, decided to keep my feminist mouth shut. The nameless Baja Bug men thanked the Saab and Citron guys, climbed into their car, waved at me and took off. I wondered what the verdict was. Maybe I should ask.

"What's going on?" I inquired in my best girlie voice.

"Well," began the Saab driver, "we decided that we can take you as far as Bahia de Los Angeles." He paused, waiting for a response.

"Okay," I answered excitedly, "They have telephones there, I think." I still wasn't sure just who I would call, but at least I would be in a primitive form of civilization.

The Saab navigator took a tool kit from the back of the car. "We have to take the wheels off your bike," he said.

"What's the plan?" I asked beginning to doubt this whole

rescue mission.

"The plan," began the Citron driver, "is to take the wheels off the bike and put them and you in the back of the Saab. Then we can strap the rest of the bike in the back of the Citron."

The Citron navigator broke in, "We'll be traveling at race speed and you won't have a seat. It won't be comfortable." He looked at me as if waiting for some sort of endorsement.

"Sounds good to me."

"You'll have to take your bag and other stuff off your bike," chimed the Citron driver.

"Maybe she can sit on it?" suggested the Saab navigator, as he removed the front wheel from Deek and began working on the back one.

"My name's Kathy," I announced, as if it mattered.

"I'm George. That's Frank. He's David and there's Ron," the Saab driver courteously pointed everyone out. They all nodded politely. Finally, some sophisticated men, well... at least polite.

The crew was so quick; they could have been a pit-crew for NASCAR. They tied Deek's carcass on the back of the Citron. They were accurate in telling me that it was not going to be comfortable. Setting my sleeping bag on bare metal and hanging onto the roll cage, I climbed into the back of the Saab. Ron placed one of the wheels of Deek on my lap. The other wheel was tied to parts of the roll-cage.

"All set?" inquired George rhetorically as he turned the ignition key.

51

"Yep."

Away we went. I surmised the sleeping bag would pad my butt enough to protect me from continuously crashing into the roll cage and metal framework. I was wrong! The wheel in my lap soon became heavy with the spokes repeatedly bruising my knees. Every bump or dip in the road hurt and there were thousands of them. I felt as if I was a tin can bouncing at the end of a rope.

After an hour we came to a stop under some tall bushes. Frank offered me a drink of water. I gratefully accepted. As I drank, a puzzled look gradually came over Frank's face. It finally occurred to him to ask how I became stranded. After relaying my tale of woe, I received many condolences.

"What kind of friends do you have?" asked George.

"Not very good ones," was my answer. All agreed.

The break was short as the sun had begun to enter the second half of the sky and we still had miles to go just to get to the half-way point. Another hour and a half and we were in Bahia de Los Angeles. I was glad to have met my quadrille of heroes, but equally glad to get out of that Saab. My butt, knees, shoulders and elbows were bruised from banging and bouncing about, but I did not complain. I knew they would heal faster than the animosity I had felt for my "friends." I was finally in civilization – well, sort of.

My four heroes unloaded Deek, replaced the wheels, and bid me farewell. I will forever be indebted to them. Now, how to get the remaining 150-plus miles from Bahia de Los Angeles to Ensenada? Step two, or was this step three or four? I'd lost count.

The welcoming cantina situated on the point at LA Bay filled the air with the aroma of heavenly food. The dirt surrounding the cantina was chockfull with off-road vehicles from dune-buggies and trucks to racers and motorcycles. Maybe the cantina would have a phone. Anyway, who was I going to call? As I approached the entrance, a howl of conversation and laughter spewed out the open door. Wiping filth and sweat from my face, I entered and the room fell silent. The patrons were muck covered, grubby and weather-beaten. If they were only sporting cowboy hats, one would think I had fallen into 1860. A woman alone in a cantina, miles from civilization, is a curiosity. For a woman to be pre-running the Baja 500 on a motorcycle during the '70s was totally out of the ordinary.

A waitress behind the counter pointed out a seat for me at the bar. She smiled and asked, in broken English, what I would like to eat. I ordered an enchilada and a Coke. I was served a cold taco and warm beer. It didn't take long before I was enjoying the concern for my situation and the frowns of disapproval at my friends – or acquaintances - abandoning me and the nods of appreciation at my rescuers. I was the queen of the cantina – a grimy, scraggly queen, but none the less, royalty. I relished the attention. Finally the conversation turned to "what are you going to do now?" I had no idea.

The answer appeared in the form of four pickup trucks and eight men ranging in age from early twenties to late forties. One of them had overheard my whining while gulping a couple of cervezas. He discussed it with the others. There was evidently some dissention among the troops, but in the end I won. *Or did I?* One must realize that had I been known for making wise decisions I would not have found myself in this dilemma. Adventure! I loved adventure. However, the options at this point were somewhat limited.

They loaded Deek and my gear in the back of one of the trucks. Only two of the trucks had a bench seat in the cab, the others had bucket seats. A quick discussion took place and I was pointed in the direction of the unfortunate duo that had been elected to drag me along. They had agreed to take me as far as San Felipe. From there, I would be on my own again. But at this point, hopping from town to town, bump to bump, and dirt road to dirt road back to Ensenada was most suitable. Still on the east coast of Baja, San Felipe would be about a third of the way to my ultimate destination.

Although my ride had a bench seat, it did not have center seat belts. Bracing myself with my feet against the floor, I straightened one arm with my hand on the headliner and pushed up to keep from bouncing around too much. It was exhausting as we were again traveling at close to racing speed. But, I kept telling myself that I was inching my way back to Ensenada and my poor lonely little Chevy LUV truck. After a few miles, it became apparent that the navigator, a thirty something whom I will call Jerk, had over-indulged back at the cantina.

"Hey, I don't see a ring on your finger. You married?" Jerk slurred.

I hesitated and replied, "No."

"You got a boyfriend?"

I paused. If I said no, then I will be leaving myself open for solicitation of favors. I lied, "Yes, I have a boyfriend."

Jerk grumbled in gutter-slang about how it must not be a serious relationship or I would not be traveling alone. Talk came around to questions about what a nice-girl-like-me was doing in a place like this. I wondered myself.

Jerk began "accidentally" falling in my direction when we hit a bump. This occurred about every other second. Then occasionally he would grab my knee and say, "Oh, I'm sorry," as he squeezed it and smiled sarcastically through crooked tobacco stained teeth. It became a long annoying trip.

The sun had dwindled and it was dusk when we finally arrived at a gas station just south of San Felipe. It took me a few moments to fall painfully out of the cab of the truck. I was stiff and sore from way too many miles of bouncing and crashing around. I examined Deek. My motorcycle had traveled very well. The guys had it tied down so tight that it didn't budge during the violent trip.

"Well, I guess I'd better unload my bike," I said to the driver of the truck I will call The Duke. He seemed to have manners. I wondered why he had chosen those slobs for traveling companions.

"Let's leave it for a while until we find out how you are going to get to Ensenada from here," suggested The Duke. I nodded. I did not want to be overly anxious to depart from my current knights.

While the trucks were refueling, I found the ladies room complete with a toilet that had been plugged with feminine hygiene products for what smelled like weeks. The toilet had overflowed more than once. There was only half of the lock left on the door and a burnt out light bulb dangling precariously from a ceiling fixture. Enormous bugs ran off in several directions when I turned on my small flashlight. I had spent several years working in construction and learned to use the most untidy facilities without touching anything. I would have preferred a nice clean bush.

When I rejoined the group, they had made a decision. Since they had my bike loaded and since we were all headed in the same direction, they had agreed to give me and Deek a ride all the way to Ensenada. This was, of course, if I was agreeable. It took a nanosecond to assess my choices, which were slim and none. I could try to hitch a ride with some other strangers, or walk, pushing my broken bike for a hundred plus miles, or take them up on their offer and ride with the strangers with whom I was gradually becoming acquainted. To know them was, not necessarily, to love them. But, I thanked them copiously and agreed to the ride.

"We were planning on camping in the desert west of San Felipe," The Duke stated skeptically.

"Sounds fine to me," I said straining to sound keen on the idea. Jerk grinned, not unlike a pedophile.

We ate at a local cantina. Beer and tequila seemed to be the only beverages available. The water was not palatable.

The beer was warm – the tamale cold. It tasted good. I was hungry.

Across the pot-holed street was a small liquor store where I was able to find some Cokes in bottles to take with me the next day. It was Sunday evening. I had thought that I would be home by now. I was glad I had told Grandma and Karen that I might not be back until Monday.

At the cantina, the group was getting ready to explore the rest of the town. I was afraid to let them out of my sight. They held all the cards. It was then I realized I didn't know any of their last names and some were called only by nicknames like Skip, JJ and Buddy. I reached in my backpack and pulled out my pencil and notepad; the one with my last will and testament. I wandered around to the back of each pickup, jotted down the license plate numbers and put the paper in my pocket. The names I would write down later. My reasoning was if the authorities found my body, I might be able to posthumously give them a clue that would lead to the perpetrators. *No, they wouldn't hurt me. Too many witnesses....*I hoped. With the exception of Jerk, they all seemed to be somewhat reasonable people.

I spent the evening dutifully trailing behind my knights up and down the main street of San Felipe. We hit every bar and Jerk had a beer or shot of tequila in each one. The group met several friends, also pre-running the racecourse. All the while, I searched for some of my own friends I knew had been planning a Baja weekend. The town was crammed full of racers and other tourists. Finally, I recognized people from the Southern California desert races. I didn't know them well.

"Hi, how are you guys doing? You here pre-running?" I asked trying to make small talk before pleading for a ride.

"Yeah," the older guy answered. "You pre-running? Who you with?"

It was the opening I was waiting for and the perfect lead-in for my pathetic story. I explained my dilemma and waited for them to offer me a ride.

"Wow," one of them said sympathetically. "Sure wish we could help."

"Me, too," I said in anticipation. They didn't offer anything. Total silence. So I mustered up all my intestinal fortitude and asked, "Could you give me and my bike a ride to Ensenada?"

"Gee, no," came the answer apologetically. "We only have our bikes. We left our trucks in Ensenada, too. We'd help if we could, but…" His voice tapered off.

"I understand." I bailed him out of the awkward situation. "Thanks anyway." Then in an afterthought, "Do you know any of the other San Diego racers down here?"

They mentioned a few names of other people they had seen, but they had all headed out all ready. Looks like I was stuck with The Duke and his hairy men.

I caught up with my liberators once more. It was midnight. I was exhausted. I'd had a very busy day. Finally the group decided it was time to find a suitable place to crash for the night. We hopped, or in my case, crawled back in the trucks and headed west. About a mile or so out of town was a hard-packed wash where several other groups had set up camp. We caravanned into the area and the trucks pulled into a circle like covered wagons preparing for some sort of inevitable attack.

Where was I going to sleep? I had thought that I would just climb into the back of the truck carrying Deek, but it was full of tools and gas cans. The Duke was not about to unload all that gear just for me. I would have to sleep on the ground. I was currently a member of the San Diego Mountain Rescue Team and had been trained in wilderness survival. I had slept in a snow cave in the Sierra Nevada Mountains and on a red-ant nest in the Cuyamaca Mountains. I had even been a Girl Scout. I could handle another night on the ground. At least, I thought I could. We heard shrieking from a neighboring camp. Something about a scorpion bite. Then another neighbor told us about the snake he had seen earlier. I draw the line at snakes, scorpions and, yes, even lizards. I am not a reptile kind-of-gal.

At times, I have been called a wimp, a whiner, and even a "silly girl". I admitted to being all of the above, especially the girl part. I saw something squiggling into a bush. The creepy slithering critters now made it impossible for me to even consider sleeping on the ground. Then Jerk offered me his cot. There was a problem with his generosity. His foul, sweaty, disgusting and raunchy body was part of the bargain.

"No thanks," I said firmly.

In his drunken stupor, Jerk kept at it. His offer became

more physical. I pushed him away and again firmly told him "No." Over indulgence in Mexican beer caused the group to laugh at the slightest thing. My refusing the amorous advances of their romantic friend set them all in hysterics. This embarrassed and angered Jerk. He grabbed my arm, pushed me to the ground and fell on top of me. Due to his drunken state, I was able to shove him off and scrabbled to my feet. Now, I was angry. I used words and called him names my mother, and even my father, told me never to say and I cannot repeat as a mature adult. They seemed appropriate at the time.

"But, Baby," Jerk slobbered as if the word "baby" was supposed to make me melt into his filthy arms. "But, Baby. I just want a little lovin'."

I used a few more choice words and again Jerk became angry. This time, his buddies pulled him back and tried to calm him, telling him I wasn't worth it. *Not worth it? Thanks a lot, guys.* My ego damaged, I was still indebted. Jerk slurred some obscenities in my direction and promised to "get a piece of my ass" at a later time.

The Duke pointed to his truck and suggested I sleep in the cab. I enthusiastically took him up on the offer. As I climbed in, rolled up all the windows and locked the doors, I could see Jerk puking his guts out on his cot – the eternal romantic. How could a "baby" like me resist such a virile specimen?

The night temperature in the Baja desert in late May was in the nineties. It was stifling in the front of the truck and the bench seat had a bump in the middle making it impossible to lie flat. I was not complaining. It was the safest spot around. Okay, maybe I was complaining. But, mostly about the imbecile who allowed herself to get into this predicament.

The heat and my stiff aching body became unbearable. I rolled the windows down about six inches to allow some cross ventilation and managed to doze off. I had slept only a few minutes when I felt a hand on my head. I sat up with a start and was suddenly being pulled toward the window by my hair. I screeched partly in shock and partly in pain.

"Let me in, you bitch!"

I recognized the seductive slurring voice of my amorous friend.

"Let go of my hair!" I screamed.

"You let me in!" Jerk insisted.

I could see that this conversation was going nowhere. He wouldn't let go and I couldn't let him in if I wanted to. He had me by the hair so close to the door that I couldn't open it.

"Okay okay," I yelled in pain. "I'll let you in, but you have to let go of my hair."

The idiot fell for it. As soon as he let go I rolled the window up and scooted to the other side of the cab and rolled that window up before he could stumble around the truck. He was livid and cursing me with his entire vocabulary of obscenities. Being some village's missing idiot, he knew only one. It started with an "F." Realizing he'd been rejected again, Jerk started kicking the doors and pounding the windows with his fists. This was a mistake.

Now he had the undivided attention of the owner of the truck. The Duke was not a happy man. He flew toward his truck with Skip and JJ at his side. Jerk found himself being slammed to the ground. The Duke was screaming about his truck being dented. Jerk was trying to explain through muffled vocalizations. Jerk was now rolling on the ground complaining of an injured knee. *Like who cared?* I was hoping for something a little higher to be injured. The Duke didn't care either. He was still upset over his dented doors.

Deciding that the truck cab was still the safest place for the time being, I watched the excitement outside. Soon, Jerk had been pushed back to his cot with dire threats of bodily harm if he moved again. The Duke and the others stumbled back to their respective cots mumbling something about it all being some "broad's" fault. I was led to believe they were talking about me. *What did I do? Poor innocent me?* Oh, yeah. I came on this stupid trip. That's what I did.

Confident the doors were locked; I rolled the windows down about two inches to keep from suffocating and tried to get some more sleep. I finally dozed off to the reassuring sounds of Jerk regurgitating.

The morning sun was still at least an hour from poking its sleepy head over the horizon when I quietly opened the door to look for that all-important bush. I found my natural toilet and felt like a human being again. The rest of the group was just opening their blood-shot eyes. Jerk moaned and groaned and staggered to his feet. He never made eye contact with me again, not that morning or for the rest of the entire trip.

Ignoring an embarrassing situation is one way of suffering through it.

Skip opened a stale bag of pretzels and graciously offered some to everyone. Stale pretzels and a warm Coke made a delightful breakfast. Bags were packed and stuffed into the back of trucks. We were ready to hit the road. With little conversation, I was pointed to The Duke's truck and Jerk to a different one. Our new traveling companion was Mr. Nice Guy. *Whew! What a relief.*

We began the long trip west toward Ensenada. The other trucks led the way and we brought up the rear. This time our speed had slowed from the day before. Our previous near racing speed was now a mere hasty drive down a country road. The tension of the previous evening activities had taken its toll on everyone. The bruises I had acquired over the past few days of being bounced around in a Saab and a truck, sleeping in ergonomically incorrect positions in the cab of a pick-up or in a sleeping bag on rocky ground were taking their toll. I was hurting. I was bushed, miserable, sore and exhausted. All I wanted to do was to be home with my daughter and my little dog.

Traveling through open countryside has its unique share of excitement. Range cattle of every size, age and sex munch grass next to, or worse, in the middle of the road. At our fast pace, this can prove quite hazardous. I braced myself at each curve praying we didn't come grill to horn with some unsuspecting bovine. We rounded a curve to find JJ running, jumping and waving his arms in warning. We came sliding to a stop.

"What's up?" shouted Mr. Nice Guy.

"That," he pointed to one of the other trucks had slid sideways into the scrub brush.

The driver of the ill-fated vehicle was climbing out, apparently unharmed, but shouting obscenities - something to do with a cow. By the side of the road were an adorable little calf and its mother wandering off into the brush, seemingly undisturbed by their close call with the "cow-angel" of death. We scrambled out to examine the situation. Thankfully the truck was not damaged. The vehicle had managed to become high-centered on a mound of dirt, wheels dangling in thin air. It was decided to tow it backwards out of the brush and off the mound. The expedience and organization with which the group performed gave me the impression these guys had done this before. Within a few minutes we were on the road again.

By noon we were more than halfway to the west coast of Baja. We had made a few quick rest stops, but now, everyone was ready for lunch. We cruised into Valle de Trinidad, a little agricultural town complete with a general store and gas station. The gas station also housed a real, honest-to-goodness, "women's room". It had a door and everything – well – not everything. It didn't have toilet paper, but I thought it was heaven compared to the bushes and the dungeons to which I had recently grown accustomed.

From Valle de Trinidad, the course climbed northwest out of the valley and into hilly and mountainous topography.

Gradually I became aware of the stench of three days' worth of body odor flowing through the cab of the truck. I realized I was contributing to this problem as much as anyone and it made me more anxious to get home and take a long shower with my luffa sponge and scrubbing crystals. I could hardly even remember my home. I missed Karen and Lillian. I reflected on how nice it must be to make "intelligent" life decisions. Maybe someday I would know first-hand how it felt. I always told myself I loved adventure. I should have been more specific.

The last sixty miles or so were on fairly good roads, at least by Baja standards. Soon Ensenada was in sight. Approaching the town from a different direction confused me. Where was my little yellow Chevy LUV truck with the flowers on the side? I knew it wasn't too far from the harbor, as I could see the water and smell the fish when I parked it there a month ago. *No, wait… it was only two days ago.*

Fortunately, Mr. Nice Guy and The Duke were more familiar with the town. After a brief description of the restaurant and the vacant lot, they seemed to know right where we were heading. The traffic in Ensenada was crazy with obnoxious gringos in their noisy race vehicles, 4x4 trucks and motorcycles. Most were drunk or acting drunk. I was embarrassed to be a considered part of this uncouth exposition. They - *we* - were truly "ugly Americans." We deserved the sordid glares from the locals.

Streets and shops were starting to look familiar. Finally we rounded a corner and I spied my LUV. It never looked better. It was covered with filth and several notes were stuck under the windshield wipers. The Duke drove over the curb onto the dirt lot. As we slowed, I nearly shoved Mr. Nice Guy out the door in my haste.

"What's your hurry?" Nice Guy asked with a chuckle. "You'd think you didn't like us."

"I must confess…I am so happy to see my truck safe and sound."

"I bet you are," chuckled The Duke.

I searched my pockets for my keys. The Duke backed his truck up to the tailgate of my Chevy. His truck was a good foot and a half taller than mine, but we were able to just turn my motorcycle around and drop it into the bed of my little truck. My tie-down straps were still under the seat and all was well with the world. Finally, both my vehicles were together. I thanked my knights for all their help, with the exception of Jerk. They mumbled a collective, "no problem," but I knew it was and I truly was indebted.

The Duke wanted to wait until I got my vehicle started to make sure I was going to be able to drive home. I appreciated that. My LUV started immediately and I waved good-bye to my knights as they drove off into the Mexican sunset. I retrieved all the notes from my windshield.

"Hope you get home okay - Tom."

"Hey Kath! I didn't know you were coming down. - Pete and Sue"

"Hey Kathy, see you at the beach. - Hank"

He was my neighbor back in Mission Beach - small

world.

"No Parking," written in Spanish. When I read that note, I was surprised that my truck had not been towed away to some obscure impound lot with a $200 plus ransom fee attached. I presumed the police were too busy with the drunks.

The gringos, aka annoying Americans, were beginning their trip home. Many were racing through the streets shouting obscenities to their friends and littering the streets with empty beer cans. The vehicles, as well as their drivers, showed the battle scars of the rough roads just traveled. All in all, I felt lucky. My truck was still intact, my motorcycle was repairable, although it was going to cost me that old pretty penny, and I still had my self-respect. The trip north to Tijuana was uneventful. I could only hope that I had learned from this blunder. I needed to be more precise about my adventuresome nature.

Upon arrival at the United States border crossing, I was confronted with a four-hour wait. Friendly motor home owners allowed us to use their facilities while stopped in a seemingly infinite line of vehicles. Eventually, I was allowed entry into the good ol' USA. *Hooray!* Traveling north on Highway 5 seemed surreal. Other motorist who did not spend their holiday weekend hitchhiking out of Mexico appeared to be content on their way home from Grandma's or a picnic or some other family outing. I was envious as I drove toward Crown Point and the aroma of fresh ocean air.

Arriving at Grandma's house, Karen ran out to welcome

me. Tears and smiles filled my greeting as I was elated to see her. Lillian wiggled and wagged her canine hello. Grandma came out on the porch.

"How was the trip?" Grandma asked.

"Fine. It was fine...very interesting."

Grandma noticed my watery eyes.

"Are you all right?"

"I'm fine. Just some dirt in my eyes."

Karen hugged me and then pulled back. "Mom, you stink!"

I smelled my armpit. She was right. Three days of heat and filthy roads had left a repulsive aroma. My hair was matted and sweaty from helmet wear. Even the dog kept her distance.

"I'll be glad to take a shower as soon as we get home."

"I hope so," she responded, wrinkling her nose.

The next day after dramatizing my escapade to my associates at work, a friend approached.

"Hey, a bunch of us are planning a motorcycle trip to Mike's Sky Ranch in a few weeks. You know, down in Baja. Wanna go?"

"Who's going?"

He ran through the list. I didn't hear the names Puch, Tom, or any of those scoundrels.

"Yeah," I said, "Sounds like fun."

Tanks a Lot

By 1975, I obtained my first job as a truck driver. I operated the fuel tanker, an ugly motor vehicle about the size of a UPS delivery truck with four tanks: 500 gallons of gasoline; 300 gallons of diesel; one tank for motor oil and another for radiator water. Most of the evening employees worked in the comfort of the garage enjoying the companionship of other mechanics and helpers. The tanker driver drove alone from dimly lit yard to dimly lit yard, occasionally confronted by a shabbily dressed homeless alcoholic looking for the Detoxification Center located a couple of blocks away. It was an isolated and lonely job.

The mid-seventies was a time when the country was slapped in the face with the realization that it was foolishly dependent on foreign oil. There were long lines at gas stations and people began siphoning fuel from their neighbors. Thus the locking gas cap was introduced. SDG&E installed locking gas caps on all company automobiles and light trucks.

This created a bugaboo for the tanker operators. When parking in a secured lot, the driver of each vehicle was supposed to either unlock the gas cap or leave the keys in the vehicle. Many employees forgot to do either. This created another problem – the hunt for spare keys or leaving a note notifying the driver that their vehicle had not been refueled.

In the small urban area neatly tucked at the east end of Mission Valley along the San Diego River is the community of Grantville. It was one of the outlying facilities for which I was responsible and where the majority of the meter-readers were located. Meter-readers had a dangerous job. With utility rates climbing, these poor employees were subject to being sprayed with hoses, dog attacks, and even threatened with guns by customers who did not want to pay for a product they used. The parking lot at Grantville was not fenced, so a security guard was appointed to keep an eye on the facility and the vehicles. All the cars had locking gas caps. The keys were kept on a board in the office in numerical order by vehicle number. The routine was to wake up the security guard, who was sleeping in his car. The guard would let me into the office. I would fill my jacket pockets with car keys, proceed to fuel the vehicles and upon completion return the keys to their proper place.

I had developed a system. The fueling hose was quite long. I determined that if I parked the tanker between eight cars, all parked at an angle, I could fuel all eight without having to move the tanker. I would locate the proper key, unlock the cap, insert the nozzle and begin fueling. On cold nights I would put the nozzle on automatic, meander to the front of the tanker and lean against the warm cozy radiator, sometimes dozing off, until I heard the familiar click indicating the nozzle had shut off and that car was full. Then I would move onto the next vehicle and resume my nap.

It was one of those nights when I was extremely tired and bored. It was late spring and the evenings were beginning to indicate the warming trend of the summer to come. After fueling all the vehicles, I removed my jacket and tossed it on the seat of the tanker. I returned to the Auto Repair Shop, turned in my time slip, grabbed my jacket and drove home.

My shift ran from 4:30 PM to 1:00 AM. Some of the second-shift employees talked about how they would have to "unwind" at the end of the work period. They bragged of watching late night TV or making a snack or other such relaxing activities. I was not one of those people. I arrived at my La Mesa condo at 1:30 AM, thanked and dismissed the babysitter, and was in bed asleep by 1:45.

This particular night, I thought I heard an odd sounding "clinky kerplunk" when I tossed my jacket onto the chair by the door. My jacket, also, felt unusually heavy. I chalked it up to being tired and weakened from a long day. The sound and the weight lingered in my semi-unconscious mind as I snoozed. Suddenly, I sat up in bed. My eyes opened wide and looked at the clock. It was 3:22 AM. I realized what the clinking sound was.

"Oh, crap!" I said, startling Lillian and making the innocent sleeping dog jump.

The clink was the sound of keys in my pocket – company keys – lots of them. With Lillian following, I ran downstairs and grabbed my jacket.

"Oh, my God!" I groaned as I dumped the keys onto the floor. "Oh, crap! Oh, my God!" I repeated as if repetition could solve the problem. I slumped on the floor and whined, "What am I going to do?"

Lillian stared at me like a good dog, patiently awaiting

instructions to help ease the tension.

The meter-readers started work at 7:00 AM. I looked at the clock – 3:27. I could take the keys back to Grantville. The security guard would be there. But what about Karen? She was upstairs sleeping. She started school at nine and I normally arose at 7:30 so I could fix her breakfast, her lunch, kiss her goodbye and she'd walk to school. Then I would go back to bed for an hour or so. After discussing the situation with Lillian, I decided to wake Karen at six, put my jammied daughter and the dog in my little truck, race through morning traffic, and deliver the keys to Grantville before any early-bird supervisors reported to work. I reset my alarm for 5:45 AM and unsuccessfully tried to go back to sleep.

I turned off the alarm seconds before it made its obnoxious racket. Grabbing what clothes were easily available, I got dressed, got my lethargic sleepy daughter out of bed and told her I'd explain on the way. The three of us climbed into my Chevy: me, Karen, and Lillian.

I darted in and out of traffic like those people at whom I usually wave a middle finger. As we came sliding to a stop in front of the door at the Grantville offices, I spied a suit and tie guy approaching.

"Are you one of the supervisors here?" I inquired, attempting an innocent sounding voice.

He confirmed and I regurgitated my tale of woe. He winced as I produced the "stolen" keys and asked if I could return them to the keyboard. He then noticed Lillian and a pink-robed squinty-eyed nine-year-old waiting in my truck.

"Isn't it a school day?" he scowled at me as if I was a bad mother. I felt like one.

"Yes," I replied, "we'll be rushed, but she should make it on time."

He relieved me of the tangled pile of keys and instructed me to get home.

"Thank you, sir."

"And don't let it happen again," he shouted as I drove away. I nodded and waved.

The meter-reading supervisor was a forgiving man. When I returned to work that afternoon, I expected to be summoned to my supervisor's office for a well-deserved reprimand, but I never heard anything about my little discrepancy. So, reassured, I went back to the "boring" job of refueling.

Fore!

Due to an economic slow-down and company layoffs - which I missed by one week of seniority - I had tanker duty for nearly three years. Typically, it was only six months. The process of filling up the small vehicles seemed to move right along. Their tanks only held fifteen - plus or minus - gallons. But filling the larger trucks and work equipment could be a tedious undertaking. Some of the big trucks had two fifty-gallon diesel tanks, one on each side. The majority of the big guys were parked in a large round lot called "The Hole" a couple of blocks from the main facility. In a previous life, The Hole had held a huge natural gas storage tank. The lot was sunk in the ground with a cement wall surrounding it. A driveway had been constructed to allow vehicle entrance. It was in The Hole where I found the "fateful" golf club.

Filling up a fifty-gallon fuel tank can take a while. To amuse myself I would meander about or, if I felt extremely efficient that day, I would check the fuel tanks on the neighboring trucks. It was on one of these excursions I found a golf club leaning against the wall. It was a number one wood. I had played golf sporadically for several years, albeit not very well, but I knew how to swing a mean drive. I took a couple of practice swings. It felt good. I took a couple more. I found a golf-ball-size pebble innocently lying within reach. The parking lot was big. The diameter of the round open area in the middle was clearly a couple of hundred feet, maybe more. I wondered if I could drive that rock/golf ball across the yard.

I addressed the "ball." I took another practice swing. I wiggled my butt like the pros. I kept my eye on the "ball." I swung. It had a stunning arch worthy of the LPGA. The yard was dimly lit and I found it difficult to follow the drive. I heard a noise – the distinct sound of glass breaking.

"Oh, shit!" I groaned.

I heard the nozzle click off indicating the truck I was refueling was full. But, my attention was now focused on a possible incident which might end my short career with one of the largest employers in San Diego. I ran toward the sound. *What have I done?* I was near tears.

There were four possible victims. I studied their windshields. They all seemed to be intact. I replayed the sound in my head. It seemed like a sound of smaller glass – smaller than a windshield. I rubbed my forehead and then as my eyes refocused, I spotted my victim. Strewn about were the remnants of a headlight. I pondered why I could not be that accurate on the golf course. I picked up the broken glass and cautiously placed it in a nearby trash receptacle.

I finished fueling the vehicles in The Hole, the last lot for the night. One of my responsibilities was to report any necessary repairs on the vehicles, like missing mud flaps or, in this case, a broken headlight. I filled out a repair card with the vehicle number and the needed repair information. I tucked the tanker in for the night. With repair card in hand, I strode solemnly into the foreman's office.

Karen and I had been living in our condominium for little

over a year. *What if I got fired? How was I going to make the payments without this job? Maybe I could get two jobs, but doing what?* I already knew that secretarial work, or the politically correct title of administrative assistant, did not pay as well. I had an epiphany. *Maybe I could offer to pay for the repair myself?* I would give it a try.

The foreman, a fatherly man in his late fifties, puffed on his cigarette, looked at the card in my hand and innocently asked, "Found a problem?"

"Well," I hesitated, "yes, I did, but I can explain and maybe I can pay for the repair."

The foreman took a drag and exhaled filling the tiny office with a distasteful haze, leaned back in his chair, gazed at the ceiling and asked quietly, "What'd you do?"

I explained that I was playing with a rock and accidently broke a headlight. I decided not to tell him about the golf club. There was a pause. He stared at me with a fatherly frown, making me feel like a bad little kid.

"So," he began cautiously, "you were driving by this truck in the tanker and ran over a rock that flew up and hit the headlight."

"No, I was playing…"

He stopped me with a raised hand, as if telling a dog to stay. He repeated his statement and added, "It was an accident."

"It definitely was an accident," I enthusiastically agreed.

He took the repair card and dismissed me with a patronizing tone, "Don't let it happen again."

"Yes, sir…I mean…No, sir."

I was grateful he protected me. I was relieved. I got to keep my job, my condo and the life, and money, I had come to enjoy. I discovered later that he only wanted to avoid filling out a three-page report, but all the same, I was off the hook.

I decided to play golf only at legitimate courses.

Why I Own a Cow Bell

I wasn't lost. Not really. I knew where civilization was. I could see a highway down the side of the mountain and across a valley about fifteen miles away. But what I couldn't find was the other twenty-one people I was supposed to be with.

As a member of the San Diego Mountain Rescue Team (SDMRT), we were on a training weekend to Mount Shasta. Our objective was to climb the north face. As a child reading National Geographic, I had dreamt of climbing Mount Everest. Mount Shasta could be the precursor of that dream. It was July, 1975.

We caravanned from San Diego to northern California and the north slope of the mountain, one of the highest peaks in California at 14,162 feet. Cramming ourselves into four pickup trucks, we took turns riding in the back. They all had camper shells. They were not air conditioned, but did protect us from the sizzling July sun of California's Central Valley. The trip took eleven grueling hours including brief bathroom and lunch breaks. We spent the first night at a small camp site near the town of Weed.

The following morning we ventured to the starting point. The north side of Mount Shasta and the surrounding area was scribbled with a maze of logging roads carved in the forest. We managed to find a clearing large enough to park all four vehicles. Everyone was energized to begin this journey. Jason, Eric and Felix were the only members to

78

have experienced the climb. They became our leaders. I tied my down jacket around my waist and secured my snowshoes and crampons to the outside of my backpack. I made certain my canteen was full and grabbed my ice axe. We divided into groups and as a safety precaution, tied plastic orange trail tape, or surveyor's tape, to the trees and bushes as we made our way up the slope. This was insurance so we could find our way back through the forest to the trucks at the end of the journey.

Living at sea level in San Diego made hiking at 10,000 feet problematic. I used my ice axe as a cane to assist each and every struggling step. I was not alone. Even the macho dudes in our group were huffing and puffing.

We finally reached tree line at about 12,000 feet. It was as if someone had drawn a line in the dirt and posted a sign reading, "No trees above this point." It was incredible. We kept climbing. When you are ascending, you tend to look at the ground and occasionally up the path. You seldom peer over your shoulder to see where you have been. But Jason did and came to an abrupt stop. His eyes widened. He appeared to be in shock.

"Oh, my God," he whispered between breaths.

We turned around. It was Mother Nature that amazed him. The view was fantastic. The sky was a radiant blue and the world beneath us was clear. No smog. No pollutants. Just like it was meant to be. The trees below shimmered with the glow of fresh green branches. I hadn't noticed their radiance as I struggled past them only a few minutes before.

Kathleen McLaughlin

I pointed to a white peak lunging up through the mountain range north of us. Eric got out a map and made certain of his bearings. Jason and Eric disagreed over the name of the peak, but that did nothing to diminish its majesty. We all stood in awe. I came to the realization that there is more to life than time clocks, traffic or paperwork - there's always paperwork. Several minutes passed. No one spoke as our minds, our bodies, our spirit embraced the moment.

We all took a breath and trudged on. Base camp was to be on a plateau about nine-hundred feet from the top of the peak. When hiking up a steep mountain one must travel on a traverse trail winding from side to side. This saves energy and time. Testing the theory, I decided to try the direct route, straight up the side. I soon discovered that this method was like climbing stairs three at a time. Sensibly, I decided to follow our experienced leaders.

The climb took most of the day. Climb a few feet, rest a moment, catch your breath. Climb a few feet, rest a moment, catch your breath. I thought I was making tremendous progress, but looking back down the mountain was a disappointment. It appeared that I had not accomplished much. Tree line seemed only a hundred feet below and my path traversed only a couple of times. The more fit and experienced groups were well up the mountain. I felt defeated. My choices were continue struggling or go back to the trucks and spend the weekend alone. With encouragement from my teammates, I continued. Hours later I arrived at base camp.

Kathleen McLaughlin

Setting up camp reminded me of a preschool challenge; everyone demanding their space in the snow. No one wanted to be too close to the edge of the plateau. Since it became a first-come-first-serve venue, by the time I arrived the best spots had been claimed by the fit and famous. My choices were limited. Selecting a small semi-flat spot next to a rock protruding through several hundred feet of packed snow, I lay my waterproof mat down, my sleeping bag and my backpack. I stretched my shoulders and twisted from side to side. It felt good to be relieved of thirty pounds of stuff. The others set up tiny tents, arranged their sleeping quarters and began to discuss a late lunch. I joined them. I was hungry.

We were all responsible for our own food. Some boiled snow over small one-burner stoves to heat-up powdered soup. I was too impatient and drank my soup and tea lukewarm. Being deprived of solid food enhances your taste buds. The chalky soup was delicious.

The stress of the climb had taken its toll on the sea-level group. Most of us enjoyed the view and tried to become acclimated while several of the more "fit" scouted around for the best route to the top. By the end of the day, we had relaxed and gathered for the typical jokes, ribbing, and one-up-man-ship. As the sun slipped into the horizon it looked like one of those photos from an adventure magazine where the stately mountains glow in the silhouette of orange sky. But I was here – it was real and I was experiencing it. I regretted tossing that gum wrapper out the car window seven years ago.

The wind began to pick up and, blowing across the ice packed snow, created a wind-chill factor way below my comfort zone. Bedtime came shortly after sunset, about nine. I did not have a tent. The original plan was to share a tent with one of the other female members. Regrettably, she decided not to attend and forgot to tell me. The additional bad news was my absentee partner was the one with the tent. The only other woman on the trip was accompanied by her boyfriend. She was not about to trade him for me. Now I was going to be sleeping on the snow. I built a small snow barrier wall with snow, spread my bag out, used my backpack for a pillow, tied my boots to the pack and snuggled in for the night. It was cold. Most of the members had two-man tents. Eric felt sorry for me. After all, it wasn't my fault I didn't have a tent.

"You want to share our tent?" he asked.

"Do I what?" I was stunned. Eric was thirty-five, married and had a toddler at home. I looked at his tent-buddy, Jason. Jason rolled his eyes at me in disgust. Eric shrugged and looked at me like a perturbed parent of a teenager.

"Don't think anything perverted. It's too damn cold anyway," Eric grumbled.

"It's okay not to freeze to death," Jason commented as he tossed his gloves in the tent.

"Is there enough room?" I asked, trying to regain a sound of innocence.

"Just barely."

This was not the July beach weather I was used to in San

Diego. I weighed my options. Freeze to death…not freeze to death. It didn't take long to come up with a decision. Eric and Jason decided it would be less weird for them if I slept between. We squeezed our down sleeping bags in the tent in hotdog formation. I used my jacket as a pillow. I remained fully clothed. We all did. It was freezing and mountain climbers don't normally carry jammies. We tried our best to get comfy.

Snow is deceiving. It looks so nice and soft. Before setting up the tent, Eric and Jason diligently smoothed out a space, attempting to eliminate the bumps and lumps. They had done their best, but after a few minutes I felt like I was lying in a rock quarry. I didn't get much sleep. Jason had bad breath. It was a long night.

Grateful to see the sun, albeit very early, I struggled out of my overcrowded cocoon and performed my morning personal hygiene ritual – finding a place to pee, brushing my teeth with toothpaste and snow, and wiping my face off with a half-frozen washcloth. All my youthful dreams of conquering Mount Everest were rapidly melting.

Felix called a meeting. He had discovered a small ice cliff about a quarter mile around the side of the mountain. He thought it would be an excellent place to learn ice-climbing. Five of the members wanted to continue to the summit. The rest of us decided to stay behind. I had mixed emotions about my decision. I had come all this way and was not going to see the top of Mount Shasta, but I was excited about the opportunity to learn additional survival techniques. At this elevation on snow covered ice we were required to be tethered to one another, as a precaution. If someone slipped and began sliding down the mountain side, the others could stop them. Four members decided to stay at camp. That left thirteen of us divided into one group of four and three groups of three.

I strapped my crampons (special attachments with pointy things on the toes) to the bottom of my hiking boots, grabbed my ice-axe, put on my backpack, containing an extra sweater and lunch, consisting of crackers and beef jerky, and ventured out. I was tethered between Jason and Eric. I felt secure. The view was miraculous. A few small clouds lingered between us and tree line. Miles away miniature cars and trucks traveled on a highway that swayed in and out of the hills and valleys. I imagined myself a Greek goddess casting a spell of good fortune on the peasants below.

"Let's get going," shouted Felix interrupting my goddess' thought process.

I'm not sure if it was the altitude or the excitement, but everyone was in a giggly mood, cracking jokes, teasing remarks, smiles and grins.

"Onward and upward!" Jason shouted as if we were Argonauts. Eric hit Jason in the back of the head with a snowball. Everyone laughed and Jason made some pseudo-retaliation threats.

After hiking for half-hour, we came upon a crevasse. The dark ice canyon was about sixty feet wide. The summer sun was directly overhead, but we still could not see the bottom.

Kathleen McLaughlin

The dark hole had ragged edges and huge indentations which made me wonder about the stability of the surface I was standing on. Others had the same thought. We all stepped back. Felix took a flare from his pack.

"Let's see how deep this thing is," he said as he lit the end and tossed it. We watched with anticipation as it vanished.

"Did you see it hit the bottom?" asked Jason. No one responded. The flare had just disappeared.

"Maybe it went out," I piped in knowing I was wrong.

"Nope, it just got smaller and smaller and smaller." Felix smiled, "That is one hell of a deep crevasse." We all took another step back.

A snow bridge was just up the hill a few hundred yards. It was about forty or fifty feet thick. The bridge looked sturdy, as sturdy as snow and ice can be, but sometimes they contain pockets of air which could cave in - a disaster waiting to happen. To cross the crevasse was going to be a slow, dangerous and tense process. We divided into pairs. We belayed each other by tying a rope to one another and crossed the snow-bridge one at a time.

I was to belay Russell. That means that he would have a rope tied around him, so I could stop him if he fell. Russell was six-feet-three inches. I am five-foot-five. Russell weighed 210 pounds. I weighed 127 pounds. I liked the idea of Russell belaying me, but not me belaying Russell. He crossed first. The theory was if the bridge could hold him, it could hold anybody. Taking each step cautiously, Russell crossed. Now it was my turn.

I stood up to unwrapped my tether and reposition it. I felt dizzy and fell down on one knee. I suffered a brief spell of vertigo. Several others came rushing to my aid. I was told to sit down and rest a bit. I refused and shouted to Russell to see if he was ready for me to cross. He was. Embarrassed, I passed over the snow-bridge cautiously, but undamaged. Once everyone had crossed; we trudged over to the ice cliffs. The cliffs were about twenty-feet at the highest point and about forty-feet wide tapering off at each end. The cliff had a nice flat top and a flat base. It was the perfect training venue.

Scaling an ice cliff requires special equipment: crampons, spikes, rope and an ice axe. To climb the cliff, you first smack your axe into the ice. As Sir Isaac Newton said, "For every action there is an equal and opposite reaction." The reaction for smacking your axe into the ice is a shower of ice in your face and down your jacket and inside your sweater. The freezing shards made me gasp. Next, you reach up and screw your spike into the ice and thread your rope through it. You stab your crampons into the ice and step up. Then you insert another spike, thread the rope and reposition your ice axe, causing more ice in your face, and start over again. It was fun for about the first few steps. By the time I reached the top I was ready for a nice warm bath, a hot meal, a glass of wine and a cozy bed.

For about an hour, we climbed around, threw snowballs, belayed each other over the crevasse snow-bridge and headed back to camp. It was 2:45 PM. Felix announced that we needed to start breaking camp while waiting for the members who went to the top. Everyone began to roll up sleeping bags, dismantle tents, and load backpacks. Someone looked up the mountain and saw our summit hikers approaching. It was good timing. We were ready to head down the mountain. The summit hikers had stories to tell and we all listened, laughed, sympathized and commented. Via their stories I was informed of an easier hiking trail up the south side of the mountain with little snow and lots of hikers. I was glad, sort of, that I had chosen the more challenging route, but cerebrally filed that info in case I wanted to venture to the summit at a later date. When everyone was ready to go, Felix lectured us beginners about safety. He was good at that – lecturing – and safety. Eric explained that we were going to slide down the snow until we got to tree line. "But," he added, "be sure you have your ice axe ready in case you start sliding too fast." I nodded, remembering my ice-axe-arrest training at Mammoth Mountain the previous winter.

The ice axe is always carried when hiking on ice or snow. If you slip or fall you can build up a lot of speed sliding down a snow bank. The ice-axe-arrest maneuver is to press the axe into the snow to break and stop your slide. You need to keep your feet up so your toes with the crampons don't hit the snow and you start going end over end in a backward tumble down the mountain. That is not as fun as it sounds as I know from previous experience at Mammoth. The Mammoth trip ended with a trip to the doctor to see if my swollen hand was broken. It wasn't.

Kathleen McLaughlin

We headed down the hill. Eric, Jason and I were the last group. I observed the others as they slid down the steep banks. As I began my decent, Eric and Jason, obviously having no confidence in me, decided they should go ahead to stop me in case my slide got out of control. The first few slides went well. I started slowly, dragging my ice axe as a breaking device. What took hours to climb, took minutes to descend. Jason had reached tree line and disappeared into the woods. Eric was close behind him, but stopped to see how I was progressing.

"You're doing great," he shouted.

I smiled and watched as Eric followed Jason into the woods. I was about two-hundred feet up hill from tree line. I was getting tired. This had been a strenuous, exhilarating and arduous couple of days. I felt confident. I felt like an adventurer, like Amelia Earhart. I thought about changing my name.

Only two-hundred feet to go before vegetation. Only about a half mile to go to our trucks and only about ten miles to go before civilization and a nice meal, not one warmed over a one-burner pocket stove. Maybe even a salad, and dessert and hot coffee. I was getting carried away with my anticipated culinary experience. When… I slipped.

I plunged face first down the mountain. My sunglasses went flying as my face slid along the icy snow. Remembering my training, I rolled onto my back. The unforgiving white stuff invaded my jacket and shirt in an attempt to freeze my torso. I stuck my axe into the snow and spun around so my feet were downhill. Gasping, I hastily turned over onto my stomach, jabbed the axe deeper and slowly slid to a stop. I was just inches from the first tree. The entire event took maybe ten seconds. It felt like ten minutes. Winded, I sat up. The fatigue, the fear and the realization of how close I had come to crashing into a tree at a speed certain to cause injury had taken its toll. I started to cry. Humiliation took over and immediately I stood up hoping no one had seen me fall. I put on my big-girl panties and dealt with the situation. I realized there was an upside to my footing error. I had just descended two-hundred feet in ten seconds. I couldn't be far behind the rest of the group.

My slip and slide had taken me a little off track. After I re-adjusted my backpack, I took the first path. It seemed familiar – *or did it?* I found trail tape attached to several trees. It looked like the tape I had secured on the way up the mountain. I carefully followed the tape. Suddenly I realized that some of the tape was a dark yellow and some was orange. *What color was the tape we tied? Yellow or orange?*

"Yellow," I said confidently and followed the yellow tape.

Trees tend to look alike, especially when there are thousands of them. I shouted to find Eric and Jason. No one answered. Trees are acoustical. I shouted again. I heard the rustle of branches in the breeze, the tweeting of birds and some noises - I wasn't sure what they were - but no human sounds. All members of the SDMRT were required to wear a whistle around their neck. The sound of a whistle carries farther than a voice. I had one. I was too embarrassed to blow it. I didn't blow my whistle.

The yellow tape continued on and on. Finally the trail came to some vehicles parked at the end of a logging road. I peered through the flora and fauna and hollered. No answer. I ran to the clearing. The vehicles were not ours. They belonged to other hikers. I had mixed emotions. First, I felt remorse. *Where was my group?* Then, I felt peace. At least, I had found a sign of civilization. Through the trees I could see the highway miles away. Maybe I could still find people. They might just not be *my* people.

I followed the bumpy, jagged road exhibiting the trauma of way too many logging trucks. Spurs angled off in all directions. I took several of them only to come to another dead-end. I was frustrated, confused. The only thing I knew was that I needed to keep heading downhill. One might think this was a no-brainer, but the verge of panic causes gross miscalculations. At least I was remembering what I had learned from survival class. I wasn't panicking yet, but, again, I was feeling like Amelia Earhart. However, I decided not to change my name.

Evening comes earlier when in the darkness of pines. Glistening through the heavy forest, the sun created a glaring bright light of brilliant white on the snowy peak behind me. It seemed mocking, daunting and ridiculing. I was determined the mountain would not win. I stood erect in my Superwoman pose and marched on. It had been nearly three hours since my slide down the snow. It was getting dark. I was exhausted and famished. I still had some crackers and beef jerky in my backpack, but I decided to hang on to them. After all, I thought I might be out here all night. I grudgingly trudged on.

What was that? Voices? I heard voices. I stopped. I listened intently and heard voices again. As I began to shout, I paused. *What if it wasn't my group? What if it was some other hiking group?* Several groups had hiked past our camp near the peak. If I shouted and some other group responded I would be embarrassed. I would have to tell them I was lost. I weighed my choices of dying on the side of the mountain or dying of embarrassment.

I bellowed, "Hello!"

"Hello!" a voice responded.

"Hello!" I yelled again. My eyes watered. I was saved! With renewed energy, I trotted up the logging spur from where the voices came.

"Who are you?" the voice asked.

"Hello!" my voice was weak and hoarse. I saw vehicles through the forest. *Our vehicles!* I rounded a bend and there they were - all twenty-one of my people.

"Where the hell have you been?" shouted Felix worried.

"We waited for you on the trail, but you never showed," scowled Jason equally concerned.

"I followed the tape," I said innocently.

"Our tape?" asked Felix.

"Well, I thought it was. It led me to some vehicles," I bowed my head in shame, "just not ours."

I looked around and saw that many of the members were still in their hiking gear. *Oh, my God!* They had been organizing a search for me. Some mumbled comments that they were glad I was all right. Others grumpily pulled their gear off in disgust.

"Why didn't you blow your whistle?" someone remarked.

"I don't know." Shrugging my shoulders, I bowed my head waiting to be admonished.

"Let's put our stuff back in the trucks and get out of here. I'm hungry," grumbled Eric. Everyone agreed.

I was pointed in the direction of the vehicle in which I was to ride and climbed in. The others in the truck rode quietly down the pot-holed logging road to a cafe on the highway below. When we reached the café, I sat at the far end of the table – away from judgmental eyes and ordered a chicken-fried steak, baked potato, mixed vegetables with an ice tea. It was scrumptious. The dinner conversation, to my relief, ignored my blunders and discussed the climb, the adventure, the fun and the excitement of the trip.

We drove south for a couple of hours before deciding on a camp site. Spreading out my sleeping bag, I fell asleep instantly, as did everyone else. The following day we drove back to San Diego and back to a nice warm bed, good food and my beautiful daughter.

In January of the following year, the SDMRT held their annual awards banquet. Awards were given out for various levels of dedication. After all the honors were awarded, the announcer introduced Felix who had an additional presentation.

Felix began, "Certain members of this organization require special attention. It seems as if one of our newer members has difficulty following the proper path."

I looked around wondering to whom he was referring. I noticed a few eyes on me. I smiled an acknowledgment and continued searching.

"We have a special award for Kathleen," Felix proclaimed. I was astonished. He motioned for me to come to the front. I shook my head. Other members smiled and helped, or forced, me out of my seat.

He grinned, "I would like to present this 'Cow Bell' to Kathleen so we can all find her the next time she gets lost."

Red-faced, I thanked him and the audience, accepted my beautifully painted cowbell and humbly ate dessert.

A Hole in One

On the plus side Keith, a twenty-two-year-old hard body built like a gymnasium, was a good, reliable and resourceful coworker. On the minus side, Keith was inquisitive. Sometimes, an inquisitive employee is a benefit to a corporation. They are curious, learn quickly and can be promotable material. But, Keith just got himself in trouble.

We had both been promoted to Vehicle Operator A and had advanced past the fuel tanker "B" position. We were now delivering vehicles of all sizes to and from Auto Repair Shop (ARS) and the district garages. Still on the night shift, we worked together frequently. It was one of these evenings when the infamous hole was discovered.

Keith was assigned to deliver a crew truck to the Dells Operating District about three miles away. I was to follow in a car, pick him up and return to ARS. Keith climbed in the truck, I got in the car and off we went. We had driven only a few blocks when Keith made a spasmodic, jerky left turn at a corner. He made another spasmodic, jerky left turn at the next corner and another.

"Where is he going?" I thought wondering why he was driving so weird. I followed him as he made still another spasmodic, jerky right turn. We had rounded the block and were now headed back to ARS. I determined something must be amiss with the truck. I was wrong. Something was amiss with Keith.

The truck had a hole in the dash board where a faulty

94

cigarette lighter had been removed. The company, saving money and deterring employees from smoking, decided the lighter was not necessary and chose not to replace it. Keith wanted to see if his finger would fit in the hole. It did. It fit snuggly - too snuggly. Keith couldn't get his finger out. Unfortunately he performed this mishap while driving. He was forced to steer and shift with one hand which accounted for the spasmodic, jerky turns. The Garage Foreman upon discovering why we had returned so quickly shook his head with a combination of disgust and amazement. He motioned for one of the older mechanics to bring some grease. The lubricant worked and Keith was a free man.

Back to the Dells we headed. Arriving at our destination, Keith pulled the truck in front of the garage where the mechanics were busy drilling, hammering and clanging away. One of the mechanics approached the driver's side, opened the door and was chatting with Keith. I stopped the car and waited for Keith to join me for the return trip. It seemed the conversation was dragging. Then the mechanic began to laugh. Curious, I got out to see what was so funny. By the time I reached the truck, several other mechanics and the foreman had joined in the hilarity.

"Keith, let's go. We have three more vehicles to deliver tonight," I reminded him as I approached.

Keith looked at me and dropped his head in shame. As I rounded the door, I could see into the cab. I looked at the mechanics and back at Keith. I joined them in hysterics. In explaining why we were late, Keith demonstrated the absentee cigarette lighter incident. His finger was stuck again. A little grease and a lot of humility "unstuck" Keith. The foreman asked us to wait a moment. He disappeared to his office and in a jiffy returned.

"Here, maybe this will keep it from happening again." He was carrying a wine cork. The cork was a tight fit and with a couple of taps from a hammer it was strongly secured. I wondered why there was a wine cork in the foreman's office.

"Now, don't be sticking your fingers where they don't belong," the Foreman smiled and retorted in a patronizing tone as he patted Keith on the back. A few more minutes of ribbing and Keith and I were on our way back to ARS.

"Don't worry," I whispered, "I won't say anything."

Poor Chickens

Bubba, as we called him behind his back, was an enigma. He was tall, twenty-eight years old, with mousy-brown hair, a thin spotty beard, and smelled like he hadn't taken a shower since the last heavy rain. He had a pilot's license and was a good mechanic, both require some intelligence, but somehow he missed out on common sense. Bubba was raised in the hills of some southern state and exhibited a bit of a drawl. His sense of humor made even the toughest mechanic cringe.

Shortly after losing his pilot's license for dropping dead chickens on the home of a neighbor he didn't like, he spent the weekend in jail for using a bus stop sign for handgun target practice while an elderly couple waited for public transportation. At work, a few weeks later he approached me with a rabbit cuddled in his arms.

"Want to pet him?" Bubba asked with a cynical grin.

I declined, noticing the smirk on Bubba's face and a drop of blood on the rabbit's nose. Carlos, an animal lover, reached to pet the blank-eyed creature. As Carlos extended his hand, Bubba pulled the decapitated rabbit's head from beneath his arm.

"Gottcha!" Bubba chortled as Carlos shot back nearly losing his balance.

"You son of a bitch," Carlos grumbled and stomped back to his work station.

Other mechanics turned away in revulsion. I made a hasty

exit before I vomited my recently eaten peanut butter sandwich into the bushes behind the shop.

Bubba didn't report for work one day, which was not unusual. His wife called stating that he was filling out paperwork (there's always paperwork) at the police station. A common question amongst coworkers was "*Now* what did he do?" Gophers were destroying plants in his backyard. Being a welder, Bubba owned a collection of welding tools including a tank of acetylene gas. Deciding to rid his yard of the destructive creatures, he pumped the flammable gas down the gopher hole, waited a few minutes and tossed in a lighted match. Bubba blew up his and both neighbors' backyards.

Men are notorious for daring and challenging one another to accomplish ridiculous feats. As a child, I recalled many boys getting into serious situations because they had been "dared" - especially if they had been "double-dared." As some boys, or men, get older, they don't automatically mature. Bubba had mentioned that he could bite off the head of a live chicken. Some coworkers dared him. That was sufficient. The event was to take place on New Year's Eve. The night foreman was lenient on these special holiday evenings. After the necessary work was completed, we were hanging around the garage discussing New Year's resolutions, conducting idle chatter and nibbling on leftover Christmas cookies.

"I'll be back in a minute," Bubba said as he rushed out to his pickup truck. He returned with a live chicken.

"What are you going to do with that?" asked the concerned foreman. Hearing of the challenge, he quickly instructed Bubba to "take that bird out of the garage!"

A few of the employees joined Bubba in the alley behind the facilities. I was not one of them and there were several others who did not want to see the decapitation encounter. In a few minutes one of the younger men returned looking pale. Another man rushed to the restroom convulsing with his hand over his mouth.

"Did he do it?" I asked fearing, but knowing, the answer.

"Yep, that guy's gross."

Bubba returned with the head in one hand and the body in the other. At least, that is what I was told. I managed to hide out in the ladies' room until the coast was clear.

Within a few months, Bubba, this interesting coworker, moved back to the South. He was frequently talked about, but not missed.

Touché Crochet

I abandoned my "friends" on the night crew when an opening occurred on the day shift. Creepy as they were, I had grown familiar with the night guys. The day crew was an entirely different set of personalities. It was like starting all over again with the glares, the sneers and the what-is-a-nice-girl-like-you-doing-in-a-place-like-this questions. Working the nightshift was great for Karen and me during the summer. We could go to the beach every day, kick back and relax. But during the school year, I would only see her a few minutes each day. After five years, I was delighted to be working days.

Sally worked in the parts department. She issued the mechanics the items needed for vehicle repair - spark plugs, hoses, stuff like that. Sally was in her early-forties with short curly blond hair and a heartfelt smile. A house-wifey type, she was constantly sharing recipes with the receptionist in the neighboring building. She wore immaculately pressed jeans with perfect vertical creases and her company shirt with "Auto Parts" embroidered above the pocket was impeccable. During lunch she crocheted. Sally treated me like a younger sister and I sought refuge in her camaraderie whenever possible.

"You want to learn how to crochet?" she asked as I watched intently nibbling on my jelly sandwich – I had run out of peanut butter.

"Oh, I don't know... it looks too hard," I swallowed and

took a sip of soda.

"You can do it. I know you can."

Sally handed me the yarn and the needles. Every day during our lunch break, I was tutored in the art of crochet. My first project was a shawl. It was a large white triangular piece with tassels on along two edges. It was gorgeous. Then I advanced to a bathing suit top. It was sky blue and skimpy. I wore it one weekend and became the sexiest "surfer" on Jamaica Court until the professional strippers moved in three-doors down.

As soon as I was beginning to comprehend the knits, picks and hooks, Sally, unexpectedly, had some news.

"Good news or bad news?" I asked somewhat jokingly.

"Good news," she beamed, "I've got a new position."

She had bid on a more lucrative job on the electric side of the house and was leaving the Auto Parts Department.

"Great!" I said forcing a smile. This, regrettably, led to an abrupt end to my crocheting endeavors.

So, So Tire-d

Being a woman in a field dominated by men definitely had its moments. After a few years the novelty began to wear off for the men working at SDG&E, but not for those working at other companies. Many of our jobs installing underground utilities were coordinated with developers and their contractors.

My first experience at a large development project was when I was working days at ARS. Duties included picking up parts from suppliers, delivering parts to our mechanics in the field and working on the tire repair truck. If a company vehicle experienced a flat tire, the driver would call ARS and the tire truck would be dispatched to the rescue. It was on one of these fateful days at a construction site for a shopping mall when a gas crew ran over something sharp. The dispatcher, George, called my name over the public address system. I reported to his office immediately and was introduced to Beth; she was 35, tall, attractive and wore too much make-up for the dirty job she was about to experience.

"Hi, Beth, I heard you'd joined us. Welcome aboard," I said, trying to make her feel at ease.

Before Beth could answer, George, a short fat guy who parted his hair above his right ear and combed it over his bald head, shoved the order form at me. I wondered how long his hair really was and what would happen if he was caught in a wind storm.

George, in his typically sarcastic way, said "She started

yesterday. She just finished her 'official' indoctrination. I don't have anything for her to do because she doesn't know how to do nothin.' Take her with you and get her out of my hair."

I looked at the order form; a flat tire on a crew truck. I smiled with my bottom teeth. Although I had repaired tires in the garage on the night shift, I had never operated the tire truck alone. I had only worked with more experienced drivers. I looked at Beth. She was anxious and her eyes pleaded with me to get her the hell out of there and away from George. I felt sorry for her. Starting a new job was tough enough, but having to report to a jerk like him, was over the top.

"Come on, Beth. We'll get out of here and let him get back to his real work," I commented noticing a crossword puzzle on his desk. He grabbed it and shoved it under some official looking papers.

"Thank you," Beth whispered as we walked out to the tire truck.

"Trouble is…you have to kiss-up to the dispatchers. If they don't like you they give you all the crummy jobs." It was true. Dispatchers rule our lives.

ARS held the responsibility of keeping all the vehicles running safely. Regrettably, no one wanted to take the time to train new employees. Because of my motherly instinct and the fact that a big part of me wanted to be a teacher, I didn't have a problem helping novice workers. We took our orders to the Parts Department where records were kept on each vehicle. The parts guy gave us all the info we needed for the proper size tire and rim and the correct number of lug nut holes. He wished us good luck. We loaded the fully-operational tire in the repair truck. Beth did her part.

It was a thirty-minute drive to the construction site where the crew was waiting. It was a long thirty minutes. Beth told me where she was born, where she went to school, about lost loves, divorces and how her mother was reluctantly caring for her children while she was at work. All I had asked was, "How are you today?" I realized that most of the conversation was nervous chatter and I sympathized.

"I don't know anything about changing tires," she confessed.

"Not to worry. We can handle it. Everyone has to start somewhere." I assured her, trying to convince myself.

Our crippled crew truck was at a site filled with contractors and workers. We located the truck behind a partially completed building, got out and assessed the situation.

"Where's the tire guys?" the foreman asked with a confused frown.

"We're them," I answered.

"Oh, geeze, we're goin' be here for days," he moaned. I was afraid he was right.

He frightened Beth. I lied to her and told her that they weren't all like that.

The good news was the damaged tire was an outside dual. This meant we didn't have to jack the truck up to replace it.

Kathleen McLaughlin

All we had to do was to position a large block of wood near the inside tire and drive the truck up on it. Now the outside tire would be suspended making it easier and safer to remove. The block of wood was a regular "tool" carried in the tire truck. I positioned the block and directed a crew member to pull the truck forward. He obliged. I motioned for him to stop when the outside tire was suspended. The process went smoothly.

The number of spectators grew larger as we began the procedure. All the carpenters, plumbers and electricians on site gathered for an afternoon of entertainment – us. With Beth watching intently, I removed the good tire from the back of the truck and rolled it around in position. I removed the flat and began to swap tires. There seemed to be a problem. The truck rim was equipped with ten lug bolts. The rim on the replacement tire was equipped with twelve lug holes. Our new rim was not going to work.

"Dumb broads brought the wrong tire," the foreman muttered.

To explain to him and the rest of his gang that the tire was issued by the Parts Department would have been in vain. I silently cursed the Parts guy.

Beth moaned, "Now what do we do?"

"We fix the flat."

"Oh, God," was her response sounding a like a genuine prayer.

"This is gonna take forever," grumbled the foreman, "Everyone get back to work."

Our audience slowly dissipated. Beth and I jointly breathed a sigh of relief. Now we could relax and complete the work at hand. Beth eagerly handed me tools and we disassembled the two-piece rim, removed the flat tube and replaced it with a new one. I started the compressor on the tire truck. Since there was no safety cage, I laid the repaired tire flat on the ground, hooked the hose up and stood way back. It filled with air with no problems. With Beth's meager help, we installed the new tire on the crew truck. I hopped in the driver's seat and backed the truck off of the block of wood. She assisted in putting the tools away and the wrong tire and rim back in our truck. I let her use the hydraulic lift. She beamed like a little kid learning to ride a bike. Beth had potential. I informed the foreman that his truck was repaired. He signed my paperwork (there's always paperwork) and grumbled something about us having a nice day. A few of the crew waved, smiled and gave us thumbs up. I curtsied.

As we drove off, Beth's exhilaration over her accomplishments caused me brief reminisces. I told her about some of my experiences – only the positive ones. Our stomachs reminded us that we had not had a lunch break. We decided to stop for a chocolate shake. It was my treat.

Beth worked in the Auto Repair Shop for a few months and transferred to a clerical position as soon as one became available.

Woman Behind The Wheel

We had lived in Fresno, California, for a little over a year before moving back to San Diego in the summer of 1958. My sister, Billie, had married and stayed in Fresno. Three or four times a year, Mom, Dad and I would drive north over the Grapevine and into the Central Valley to visit Sis.

The Grapevine was jam-packed with trucks filled with merchandise, produce or other consumables slowly ascending the mountain grade. In the sixties, automatic transmissions were an option and Dad was not about to pay extra for what he considered a luxury, so our car had a stick shift. This made it challenging for us to pass some of the sluggish trucks. As we were struggling by an eighteen-wheeler, I sat in the back seat admiring the power of the mammoth vehicle as we crept passed. I looked up at the driver. It was a woman! She smiled and waved. I was astonished, ecstatic and flabbergasted. She confirmed my suspicions that women could do anything.

"Someday," I said to myself, "someday."

Seeing Double

"You are going to be assigned to Miramar Yard for the next few weeks," said the dispatcher.

"Okay… why?"

"You want to be a truck driver, don't you?"

"Ah, Yes." I humored him. I wasn't as sure about my answer as I had been when I was twelve.

"Then you'll have to learn how to drive doubles."

Doubles! I was enthusiastic and panicky. I'd had driven a few dump trucks and had towed work equipment around on single trailers. Now, with two trailers, each thirty feet, plus your tractor…you got a big honkin' vehicle to negotiate in traffic.

SDG&E's Miramar Yard was the primary warehouse and storage facility for maintenance and construction material. They stocked the utility poles, overhead and underground transformers. The satellite districts would order items to be transferred from Miramar and a set of doubles might deliver to one, or as many as five districts, each day. At the districts, they would off-load their items and then reload the trailers with RFS (retired from service) material to be hauled back to Miramar. It was a continuing process.

I arrived promptly at 7:30 Monday morning. I was greeted with the usual smirks, scowls and sneers. An instructor accompanied me for a couple of days and then signed me off and turned me loose. The first week consisted of driving around the yard, loading material, and handing the vehicle over to an experienced driver to deliver. This process allowed a new driver time to obtain the skill needed to negotiate tight corners in the yard - safely away from traffic. Since the driver is ultimately responsible for their cargo, I learned how to tie down a load properly and the correct use of straps, ratchet tools and all the details. I was used to tying down work equipment to trailers, but not reels of cable or transformers. The instructor had signed me off and vanished by Wednesday. The rest of the week went smoothly.

The following weekend, I bragged to friends about my step-up in the driving world. Some were very impressed – others had a *"whatever"* attitude.

Personally Spared

While driving doubles at Miramar, the tire changing abilities I learned in the garage came in handy. As I was heading for home at the end of an exasperating day, I discovered my Chevy LUV truck had developed a flat tire. The fact that it hadn't been flat when I retrieved my lunch at noon caused me pause. My spare tire was neatly tucked under the bed of my mini pickup. I put my personal items on the seat and slid under the truck to lower the spare. As I emerged I discovered that I had become the late afternoon entertainment. It was evident that my tire had been purposely violated. Several of my co-workers had assembled to watch me struggle.

"Got a problem?" someone shouted mockingly.

I looked up, but was not able to determine which of the group had called out. All of them were smirking. I sighed, doubting if the harassment would ever end. Standing up, I curtsied, raised my fist in the air and announced in my best Shakespearian voice, "The show must go on."

Some of them chuckled. Some of them scowled. I went back to work repairing their devious transgression. Realizing I was not going to be annoyed by their presence, the crowd dispersed making comments about how they had to get home for dinner or go to a little league game. As I began to remove the lug nuts, I heard a sympathetic voice.

"Let me help you." It was Alex, one of the laborers. He was a pleasant young man about twenty, average build, but above average character. Until now, we had only exchanged salutations.

"No, I can do it."

"I know you can," he said as he knelt and picked up the wrench, "I've seen you work."

As he assisted me with the tire, he made fuming comments about his fellow employees. He assured me it would not happen again.

Taking the Leap

The second week of "doubles" training at Miramar began routinely with a couple of trips to Carlsbad and Escondido. On Tuesday, I assisted in loading a trailer with overhead transformers - those big grey cans attached near the top of utility poles. The crane operator, Gus, would hover over a transformer with a hook on the end of a cable. Walt, the ground man, would tie a strap to the hooks on either side of the transformer and to the cable. Then Gus would lift the 150 to 250 pound transformer up to the trailer where I would release the strap, wiggle and rock the transformer into place, and prepare for the next one.

Walt, wearing his everyday faded denim shirt with holes in the elbows and the same mud-stained jeans he had worn for several weeks, was a conceited man in his mid-forties. Gus was about the same age, but much neater in his attire with a plaid shirt tucked tidily in brown slacks. Gus mumbled annoying remarks every time our paths crossed. They conveyed an uneasy feeling.

The trailer was half-full with the remainder of the space to be allocated for some other type of material. One of the transformers was being stubborn and I was having difficulty getting it into position. I noticed Walt casually standing next to the trailer with his hands on his hips.

He coughed, spat and said calmly, "I'd duck if I were you."

I was puzzled, but not for long. Swinging from the crane

on the cable was one of the larger transformers. It was heading straight toward me. Cavewoman instincts took over and I got the hell out of the way. I baled off the side of the trailer landing near Walt. He smirked and glanced at Gus.

"You son of a bitch!" I yelled and took off running toward the crane. I was livid. I was outraged. I was tired of being the smiling sweet little girl who worked her ass off. I was tired of having to work twice as hard as my male counterparts to be appreciated half as much.

As I came around the trailer, Gus looked down from his lofty perch with a tobacco stained smirk. I knew the incident was premeditated. He was an experienced crane operator – one of the best. With a leap that would have impressed Superwoman, I jumped on the side of the crane. I shook my fist in his face and called him all the names even my father told me not to say. I gave him the lecture I had been shouting at my windshield every night on the way home. I professed that I would be here long after he was gone. That better men than him had tried to make me to quit. I was here to stay. "Got that ol' man?" I screamed.

The entire time I was shouting and cursing, Gus was smiling. When I finished, he stared at me for a minute, grinned and told me to get back to work. Carefully, I climbed down and glared over my shoulder. I went back to work and scowled at everyone the remainder of the day. No more Ms. nice gal!

The following morning, the yard crew nodded and grunted various greeting. Gus was the unofficial leader of this particular pack of wolves. He had been trying to aggravate me since I'd arrived at Miramar Yard a week and a half earlier. I had smiled with my bottom teeth the entire time. Gus was the type to push, push, push until you finally pushed back. The sooner you pushed back, the more respect he had for you. Even though, it took me over a week, by his standard that was an acceptable time frame.

For the next twenty years, until his retirement, we were "best" buds. Whenever I had business at Miramar, he would come sliding to a stop on his forklift and offer his usual greeting. "Hey, what the hell are you doing here? You look fatter than the last time I saw you." I would retaliate with "Shut up, you old fart. How ya doing?" He'd say "okay," smile and disappear amongst the stacks of construction material.

Plugging Away

When flat tires and trying to knock me off a trailer did not cause the desired disruption, the scumbags at Miramar became more creative.

I approached my Chevy preparing to leave for a weekend of fun and contentment surrounded by friends who accepted me the way I was. Upper management had left for the day and the only other vehicles in the employee parking lot were those belonging to a handful of degenerates. I was suspicious as most of them should have been heading home. They were fussing with items in the trunk of their cars or occupying themselves with idle chatter. I noticed they ominously kept peering over their shoulders in my direction.

I strolled around my mini pickup, nonchalantly looking for another flat tire. All four seemed to have air. I couldn't find any damage or dents or annoying items tied or taped to my truck. I braved it, climbed in and turned the ignition key. The truck started, but instantly began to quiver and shake. The engine was running rough. Then it backfired several times – KABANG, KABANG, KABANG. I turned it off. All eyes were now in my direction. Contemplating the situation, I sat for several minutes. The ne'er-do-wells stared with curled lips and leering grins.

"Doesn't sound too good," the leader of the pack barked.

"No, it doesn't," I responded trying not to sound too concerned.

As a Helper in the garage, I had acquired some

mechanical knowledge. Due to my curiosity and the patience of some of the older mechanics, I knew the answer to some basic questions as to how engines operate and what maintenance was required. I slid out of my truck and opened the hood. I stared blankly at the mechanical mini monster nestled between the fenders. Perhaps I hadn't learned as much as I thought.

"Maybe you shouldn't have bought a Chevy," shouted a Ford dude.

"No, maybe not," I smiled being determined not to give in to the conspiracy.

Leaving the hood open, I got in and started it up again. I walked around to the front and again looked intently at the engine as it wiggled, wobbled and rocked the truck. It backfired through the carburetor. I noticed one of the sparkplug wires seemed a little stretched. Another seemed to have too much slack. I shut the engine down.

I had an "ah ha" moment - an epiphany. One of the slime-buckets had switched the sparkplug wires around. The plugs were not firing in the proper order. Being a resourceful individual, I had learned to change the oil, flush the radiator, and replace sparkplugs. Some friends called me "cheap," but my determination to save dough definitely had its rewards.

This occasion was one of them. I repositioned the wires to their appropriate order and started my mini-truck. It ran smoothly. I wished the disappointed dudes a nice weekend and drove home, clinching my teeth and cursing the bastards.

Not Paid To Think

There once was a time for me
When life was as it ought to be.
The flowers, trees, a stroll by the sea;
Then, I went to work for *The Company*.

A colorful world I leave with a fight
For eight hours a day of 'black and white.'
What you say? No shades of gray?
Oh, no, not here… no, not this day.

"Now be careful," they say, "with your use of things.
Remember the budget is dangling on strings."
Dangling on strings…Boy, he's got that right,
But somebody somewhere is pulling strings tonight.

"What?" you say, "How can that be?
A company with the reputation of Thee?"
Well, I don't know… it's just a guess,
But somebody some where's got a nice little nest.

We need more money! We have to build!
We have to get our quota filled.
We need more money. We'll raise the fees!
We'll bring our customers down on their knees.

DO THESE WORK BOOTS MAKE MY FEET LOOK FAT?
Kathleen McLaughlin

Reporters say we have money to spare,
But I tell you, consumer, it just isn't there.
We say it's not there… (It's in someone's pocket.)
And so, dear consumer, to you we must sock it.

This is the story the employees hear
Year after year, after year, after year.
So I thought to myself, "If they really are poor,
Maybe I can help and open a door."

So I did some research and looked around
And some very simple ways I found
For *The Company* to save a lot of its dough.
They don't have to spend so much you know.

They can save over here. They can save over there.
I knew they'd be proud of employees that care.
So innocent, trusting, believing am I.
Off to The Man with my notes I did fly.

I handed my notes and ideas to The Boss.
He read them and smiled. (He'd been hitting the sauce.)
He smiled…no…sneered…then looked down his nose.
"Right here. In the trash is right where this goes."

My eyes opened wide in disbelief.
I had hoped to bring some financial relief.
"We don't pay kids like you to think!"
Then he smiled and smirked and turned with a wink.

118

DO THESE WORK BOOTS MAKE MY FEET LOOK FAT?

Kathleen McLaughlin

"The consumer out there has all of the bread
That *The Company* needs to stay out of the red.
We'll raise our prices again and again."
Then he belched and burped and wiped off his chin.

"What a pig!" I thought, "What a horrible swine!"
I pardoned myself for taking his time.
"That's okay, kid. Any time. Any day.
Now get back to work or I'll garnish your pay."

Build! Spend money! Whether we need it or not,
But watch Uncle Sam and let's don't get caught.
That's the motto *The Company* goes by, you know.
So drag out the checkbook and on with the *Show*.

See Dick Run

Working in construction I learned to accept grumpy. Most of the crew members were grumpy, but so were the people living and working in the vicinity of the jobsite. If our job sent us to an impoverished area of town, the residents and shop keepers would frown at us and ask how long our dirty job was going to keep pouring dust into their broken windows. When our work took us to an affluent area of town, the residents and shop keepers would glare at us and ask how long our dirty job was going to keep pouring dust on their Lamborghini. Occasionally the job was in a new housing development and the glares and complaints were minimal.

It was at one of these new development sites where I met Dick. We were never properly introduced nor even spoke to one another. Dick was the name I assigned him. Dick, a bulky bearded lumberjack type, worked for a large gravel company located in the Mission Valley area of San Diego. Most of the gravel used on this particular development came from his employer, including the material I was hauling for our underground utility installation. Our paths crossed several times and Dick would just glare or ignore me. I preferred being ignored.

One afternoon, a few minutes past three o'clock, I was stopped at a traffic light on Mission Gorge Road. I was heading back to the job with the final delivery for the day. The traffic light also served as a crossing for an elementary school. Important-looking little crossing guards adorned in yellow vests with florescent safety strips held familiar red and white stop signs. On the side street, mothers gathered their offspring and teachers waved their good-byes. My attention was on the cute kids crossing the street – carrying hand-painted art, lunch pails or jackets, boys pushing one another, girls giggling.

"Hey, bitch!"

I looked around wondering who would use such loud disgusting language in front of children. It was Dick. He was also stopped at the light heading the opposite direction. He was waving a large - very large - rubber object out his driver side window. At first, I was puzzled. I had heard of such objects, but had never seen one before. It was in the shape of an extremely oversized male member.

"This is for you, bitch!" he shouted.

I don't remember if any of the children saw his revolting action. They finished crossing the street, the light changed to green and Dick drove off with an evil grin.

The incident annoyingly replayed itself in my head. By the time I had dumped my last load of gravel and headed toward our yard, I was furious. It would have been different if he had performed his distasteful act on the job site occupied predominately by men, or if he had waved it at me while passing on the road where it would have been seen by other adult drivers, but he perpetrated his misconduct in front of young, innocent, cute, impressionable children. Dick was fortunate he was not within *this* mother's reach or he would have been singing alto for his church choir.

When I arrived at our yard, I tucked my truck in for the night, turned in my time slip and marched straight for the phone. It was 4:45 and I hoped someone was still at Dick's gravel company to answer my call. I had calmed down to the point of no longer shouting. Dick's dispatcher had the misfortune of answering the call.

"I am not one to complain to management about the inappropriate activities or comments of men when faced with a woman on the job site," I began.

"Yes, ma'am?" was his cautious reply.

I vividly explained in anatomically correct terms exactly what his employee had done before the eyes of youngsters, their mothers and teachers.

The dispatcher quietly, but repeatedly interrupted with, *"I'm so sorry," "I'll speak to our driver,"* and *"It'll never happen again."*

I went on to explain how if my name was on the side of a truck I would want my employees to be proper, honorable representatives. He agreed. *What else could he do?* I hung up confident that the disgusting episode would never repeat itself.

The following day I was assigned to the same job. Dick was not.

'Tis the Season – Pigskin, That Is

One year, I received a call on Super Bowl Sunday from a friend who was originally from Eastern Europe. She wondered if I was watching the 'the big bowl.' Not clear on American sports, she asked, "Is that the game where two men play catch with a ball and another man tries to hit it with a stick? Or is that the one where they all line up and run into each other?" A perfect description of each sport, I thought.

As the only woman truck driver and heavy equipment operator at SDG&E, I tried to give the men some space. My intentions were not to become "one-of-the-boys." There exists a fine line between being an intruder and being a loner. If I stayed away from the group, I was accused of being "too good" for them. If I hung around too much, then I was trespassing on their territory. My resolve to this predicament was to smile, say hello and keep out of the way. I generally ate lunch alone in my truck and read a book. But, I was expected to join a select group of drivers and operators for morning coffee at the company cafeteria, before we were officially on-the-clock.

The decibel level was extremely high in the cafeteria the morning after the first game of the football season. Did you see that pass? Did you see that touchdown? Did you see that fumble? *No, I didn't watch football.* They were stunned. I might have watched if the games came on Sunday night, but I was not about to waste a beautiful Southern California afternoon sitting in front of a TV.

Quickly it became apparent that if I was to enter into the conversation I needed to be more attentive to football. I shuddered. The following week, I collected some snacks, fluffed my pillow and curled up on the couch to watch the game. I lasted the first quarter. That was all I could handle. Karen and I went to the beach.

That evening I had an epiphany. The TV news was blabbing away while I prepared dinner and my daughter was setting the table. The sports report began with the highlights of the day's football games. In less than ninety seconds I saw all the critical plays, fumbles and touchdowns. It was a miracle. I watched intently. I remembered each significant play – there were about three.

The next morning at coffee, the crew was verbalizing and demonstrating with glorified hand gestures the previous day's game. I felt confident. I chimed in with "how about that game?" Then later in the conversation I added "did you see that fumble? We almost lost it there." And, "what about that pass – that was incredible, or "how about the guy that got hurt on that tackle. Hope he's back in the game by next week." It worked like a charm. Everyone thought I had become a convert to the religious sect called Pigskin Mania.

The second part of the plan also went extremely well. During the course of the morning coffee conversation, someone would make a comment about the game and everyone would laugh. I memorized it. I plagiarized it. Then later that morning, when I was working with a construction crew, I quoted the coffee crowd. The crew would laugh.

Kathleen McLaughlin

They thought I was a passionate fan. If any of the construction crew made a comment everyone seemed to enjoy, I memorized it. I plagiarized it. And I reiterated it to the coffee crowd upon return at the end of the work day.

I became an instant "teammate," although I still managed to keep a certain distance. I discovered it worked for every sport, every season, and every game - all because of ninety seconds of sports news.

Piece Pipe

The service territory of San Diego Gas and Electric include all 4400 square miles of San Diego County, a smidgen of Orange County to the north and a teeny tiny part of Imperial County to the east. The majority of the work assignments fell within those boundaries, with an occasional trip outside of that "electric" fence.

It was on one of these rare occasions I was assigned to join Allen on a trip to Fontana, California to pick up a load of large gas pipe. It was summer 1978. I had been with the company six years – six long years. The pipe that brings natural gas to a home is small, the pipe out in the street in front of that home is bigger, but the pipe that takes the gas from one community to the next is really big. It was this really big pipe the company needed.

Allen was one of the good guys. I hadn't worked with him before, but he always had a friendly smile and a good-morning nod. He was a few years older than me, tall, mustached with blond gray-streaked hair.

As we approached the truck, he asked, "You wanna drive?"

"Sure."

"Don't forget your circle-of-safety," he quietly commented.

"I always do," I said reassuringly.

The circle-of-safety was a procedure required by all company drivers before leaving for a job. It consisted of walking around the truck and trailer checking brake lights, turn signals, tire pressure and any other concerns before heading out on the road. I examined the truck. Everything was hunky-dory.

We traveled up Highway 15 to Fontana located in San Bernardino County just east of Los Angeles. It was late spring and the inland temperatures were creeping up into the 90s. We had left the yard about 8:30 AM. The travel time was about an hour and a half, but after a stop at Allen's favorite road-side diner for breakfast, it was 11:30 before we arrived at our destination.

The pipe company was located on forty acres decorated with huge stacks of pipe ranging from two-inch diameter to thirty-six inch. A couple of large barn-like buildings housed machinery where pipe was wrapped with tar and fiberglass to protect it from Mother Nature's destructive underground moisture. The yard was dry, dusty and filled with the stench of diesel fumes, asphalt and tar.

I parked the truck and trailer where Allen instructed. We sported our stylish hard-hats, grabbed our paperwork (there's always paperwork) and entered the office. The dispatcher was talking to a muscled, balding, filthy man as we walked in. They glanced up. The dispatcher took a double-take.

"Are you driving?" he asked me with a scowl of disapproval. I started to answer but was interrupted.

"Yes she is," Allen chimed in. Filthy-Man and the dispatcher locked glares. It was one of those silent male conversations.

"Your choice," the dispatcher grumbled to Allen. He looked at our papers, handed it back and gave us directions to the location of the pipe we were to pick up. "There's a few ahead of you," he scowled.

The dispatcher nodded to Filthy-Man. He nodded back. They had their own sign-language I was not privy to; however, Allen was.

"We might be here awhile," he moaned as we left the office.

As we were climbing into our truck, we noticed Filthy-Man climbing onto an articulating loader. It was designed to bend in the middle and instead of the usual bucket on the front, it had clamps. It was colossal and it could devour me, Allen and our entire truck with one gulp. We drove to our appointed aisle and waited…and waited…and waited. Allen and I watched four or five trucks get loaded and leave. We still waited. At one point Allen explained to me that sometimes it takes thirty minutes or more to load a truck. But I knew the problem was me, the woman truck driver.

Lunch time came around 1:30. We watched our monster-lift operator, Filthy-Man, climb down his ladder and head for the office. In about thirty minutes he returned and went back to work. Allen and I discussed world situations, told each other childhood stories and took a couple of short naps while spending the day in a truck in the middle of smelly pipe yard in ninety-plus temperatures. Later we noticed Filthy-Man walking across the yard.

Allen shouted, "When is our turn?"

The operator looked at his watch and shouted back, "pretty soon." So we waited some more.

Since we had stopped for breakfast, we didn't feel hungry until about two o'clock. My lunch box contained a sandwich, a banana, a box of raisins and a thermos of fruit drink. Allen did not bring a lunch. He bought a couple of sodas from the machine in front of the office, used the phone to call our SDG&E dispatcher to report our situation and returned with a smile. We shared my sandwich and I asked him why he appeared to have a sudden positive mood swing. While recounting his phone conversation his smile became bigger. Allen reported that our dispatcher was furious about the unprofessionalism of the pipe company with which SDG&E did millions of dollars of business annually. Before Allen left the office he heard the pipe dispatcher's phone ring.

"The next thing I knew we were next in line," Allen said.

I wondered why we hadn't taken action earlier. We had been waiting for over three hours. Allen explained that he wanted to give them a chance to do the right thing. He was a patient man and I respected him for it.

Retaliation has its own retributions. Filthy-Man finally loaded our truck. I had watched him load other vehicles throughout the day – several other vehicles – and everything had gone smoothly. But when he began loading us, he suddenly seemed to suffer from brain-fade. The first couple of pieces of pipe he dropped on our trailer from about four feet. Several tons of steel pipe can cause substantial damage to equipment. Allen scowled at the operator.

"Sorry," he shouted over the noise of his giant engine, "I'll do better next time." His slimy grin made me shiver even in the heat. The rest of the pipe was loaded without incident after Allen reminded the operator that it was getting close to quitting time. We tied the load down, performed our circle-of-safety and headed out the gate about 4:00 PM.

The return trip was tedious. Go-home traffic had begun and we inched along the highway. Allen and I didn't talk much. It is amazing how doing nothing for hours in a hot, dusty, smelly pipe yard can be exhausting. It was 7:00 PM when we finally arrived at the SDG&E yard. I buttoned up the truck, put the wheel chalk under the tire and filled out my time slip. I called my daughter to let her and the babysitter know I was still alive and kicking and would be home soon. Allen called his wife.

"I'll be damned," he said as he hung up.

"What's up?" I asked.

He rolled his eyes in disgust. His wife, Jan, told him three of our co-workers had called to inform her Allen was working late with the new girl driver, implying hanky-panky.

"Is she upset?" I asked genuinely concerned.

"No, she knows me better than that," he said confidently, "and anyway, I told her all about you. She's just angry at them for trying to start something."

"I'd like to meet your wife," I said.

My daughter, Karen, and I were invited to their home for a nice barbeque and pool party the following weekend. Jan, Allen and I remained friends for many years.

130

Don't Go There

"I'm sorry, but you cannot go in there. No women allowed," commanded the security guard.

"But we have to pick up a boom truck," I said in amazement motioning toward Allen sitting next to me in the passenger seat.

"Well, I don't know what you're gonna do," he said smugly, "I guess he'll have to walk." He stood with arms folded like the retired military man he was, defying us to pass.

"You gotta be kidding?" Allen asked as he leaned over to get a better look at the guard.

"Nope," came the arrogant reply, "I have orders that plainly state no women are allowed in the power plant yard."

"But… I'm an employee," I stammered.

The security guard stood his ground. Allen, my co-worker and a good friend, was furious. We parked the pickup truck in a small lot in front of the security office and went inside. Allen wanted to use the phone. We were on a mission to retrieve a large boom truck that had been loaned to the crews at the power plant and return it headquarters which was about an eighty-mile round trip.

The plant was completing construction on Unit Five. We weren't sure where the boom truck was located. It could be anywhere on the ninety-five acre Encina Power Plant. The place was jam-packed with huge buildings, equipment, a gigantic smoke stack, massive electrical towers and wires. I peered out the guard's window eager to spy our assigned vehicle. I was hoping that the size of it would make itself noticeable, but on a project like this, it appeared to be a sea of large equipment parked everywhere.

Allen had called our Fleet dispatchers and relayed the situation. He handed the phone to the guard. We could hear elevated voices on the other end of the phone. The guard stood his ground. Allen and I stared out the window. We discussed going next door to the Carlsbad Operating District to borrow a male helper or a mechanic to assist with finding the boom truck, but decided to try it on our own. Being more familiar with the work equipment, Allen thought he saw our fated vehicle partially hidden behind a large shed. He drove the pickup, solo, with the guard's blessing, to confirm his sighting so as to keep his hiking to a minimum.

While Allen was gone, the guard relaxed his military demeanor and told me why he had been instructed to ban all women. SDG&E had hired outside contractors to perform much of the work required to build Unit Five. It seems that some of the workers would invite their wives or girlfriends to join them for lunch. During spring break or summer vacation a few children would arrive to enjoy the mid-day meal with dad. It sounded like a nice family outing, but children around construction sites raised safety concerns. So the order came down from the power plant management: No women or children allowed.

Allen returned and reported the boom truck was only about a quarter of a mile away so he decided to hoof-it.

While I waited, the guard offered me luke-warm coffee and a stale donut-half left over from this morning's breakfast. I thanked him, but declined. The guard had softened and appeared to doubt the extent of his orders. He said he had never had a woman employee try to enter, but he didn't feel comfortable disobeying instructions.

When Allen and I returned to the Fleet Dispatch Office in downtown San Diego, the dispatcher motioned for us to join him in his office.

"Well, it seems you've been a pain in the ass again," he grinned.

"This time, I hope so," I responded.

While Allen and I were attempting to perform our duties with efficiency, the Fleet Manager was on the phone to the Director - just below VP - responsible for the power plants.

"You can drive into any power plant you want," snickered the dispatcher.

"Broke down another fence didn't you," grinned Allen as we filled out our time slips and prepared to go home.

"I guess so," I answered, "I was hoping there weren't any left."

Not the Look I'm Going For

The winters in Southern California can be quite nippy. The strong bitter wind off the Pacific can even make a Midwesterner shiver. It was on one of these chilly days, I mistakenly took a little nap.

I was driving a dump truck and working with a gas crew. We were digging trenches for the installation of new utilities at the future site of an industrial complex. Installing the underground utilities was generally one of the first stages of construction. The roads had been cut into the side of the hills and were being graded to create drainage by a contractor. Otherwise the area was void of humanity - or so I thought.

It was lunch time and the gang decided to play cards in the back of the crew truck. Not being a card player I begged out to give them some man-space. I was in the middle of an exciting mystery novel and decided to find a comfy place to discover who-done-it. Book in one hand and lunchbox in the other; I strolled down a bank to an underground transformer. The big green box was perfectly positioned. It faced the warm sun while protecting me from the icy wind.

I dusted off a spot on the cement with my gloved hand before removing them and stuffing them in my pocket. Snuggling up in my cozy oversized down jacket, I nibbled on a peanut butter and jelly sandwich and began to read my book. I pulled my stocking cap over my ears and nearly covered my eyes. The morning labor, a warm spot and a full tummy took its toll. Within a few minutes, I was napping;

134

actually, I was sleeping quite soundly.

The noise of laughter startled me awake. Peering through my blurry eyes, I found myself being starred at by a security guard and being laughed at by my foreman. It was ten minutes past our allotted lunch break.

"Get up, Lazy," chuckled the foreman.

I stuttered some sort of apology. The security guard starred in amazement. "Does he, I mean, she work for you?"

I gathered my book and lunchbox. "Yeah, I work for him."

The foreman confirmed. The security guard wandered off, weakly muttering to himself.

"He thought you were some homeless guy," the foreman snickered as he helped me to my feet and hurried off to tell the rest of the crew.

"Homeless guy?" I asked in vain. That was not the look I was going for. I decided to re-examine my working attire.

A Little Different

She shaved off her beard for the job interview. By the time I met Brenda, mid-spring 1979, she had been working at SDG&E for a month. The red chin-hair was being cultivated back to pre-hire days. She was five-foot-nine, shoulder-length slightly-matted auburn hair, and a touch overweight. She had large breasts with pierced nipples which she left dangling braless beneath soiled t-shirts. Brenda was a little different.

Brenda worked as a repairman - aka repairperson - in the Auto Repair Shop. A repairman was like an apprentice mechanic learning the "how's and why's" of fixing and maintaining vehicles. The ego-syndrome and the resistance to "ask directions" made some of the male repairman not as competent as Brenda. The men would take on an unfamiliar problem without asking for instructions, frequently having to start over and, ultimately, wasting time and company dollars. Brenda, when approaching a new challenge, would ask for direction, listen carefully and accomplish the task in a timely fashion. She learned quickly and was good at her job.

Some of the office women felt uneasy around Brenda and refused to enter the ladies room if she was present. She respected their privacy and stayed out of the way. The beard bothered the other women as well as the grease and grime. Brenda was a little lacking in personal hygiene. She would report to work on Monday wearing the same slimy jeans, sloppy shirt and her hands, arms and face smeared with the same grease she left with Friday night.

SDG&E always encouraged employee safety. An employee who managed to work a specified period without a lost-time accident would be honored by the company with an award, usually a ball cap, coffee mug, lapel pin or some other useless item. After a year Brenda had met the criteria. The Fleet Maintenance Manager, a superficial, arrogant suit, invited her and the Garage Foreman to his office to present the award. The Human Resources Department did all the hiring and the Manager worked days. He might have missed a golf game if he stayed late and greeted the evening shift employees. So that was not an option. He did not spend much time interacting with his subordinates and had never seen Brenda. The Foreman and Brenda entered the Manager's office. Without looking up, he stood, picked up the safety award and stepped around his desk. Then he saw Brenda. His eyes widened, his mouth dropped and his eyes darted from her breasts to her beard to her breasts and back to her beard. Brenda stood upright, pushed her shoulders back and thrust her breasts forward.

"Hey," she said, "Pick one."

The stunned Manager took a step backwards, offered a handshake at arm's length, blushed, stuttered and mumbled something about congratulations.

As Brenda and the Foreman walked back to the garage, he patted her on the back and said, "I'm sorry about that."

"Don't worry," she sighed, "I'm used to it."

The Foreman felt sorry for Brenda, so did I.

Nudie On the Floor

I was assigned to the Dells Operating District as a vehicle operator. My first day, I was greeted with the usual nods or glares; nothing special for the first week.

When an employee was assigned to a construction crew, it was generally for the duration of that particular job. Being familiar with the job, the foreman, the other members of the crew accelerated the project thus saving time and money. It was a good plan.

My first duty at the Dells was with a gas crew, installing new gas lines in a residential area. I was assigned a dump truck. The first five days went smoothly with the foreman patronizingly explaining every step of the construction phase. I was new, but not that new. I could tell the difference between a shovel and a broom. When there was down-time for the drivers, they were expected to help sweep, clean up or do other labor-intensive activities. I didn't mind. It helped the day go faster. Other drivers would pretend to have difficulties with their vehicles or just disappear.

Monday morning of the second week at the Dells, I arrived, lavender lunch pail in hand. I walked to the office to get my daily orders and, as expected, was assigned the same dump truck I had driven the Friday before. I opened the door to toss my lunch and hardhat on the seat and found a page torn from a magazine neatly arranged on the driver's side floor. It was of a nude woman in an unattractive, suggestive and lewd pose. My shoulders dropped and my mouth fell open. I had not come across this type of dissension since the garage mechanics several years earlier. I thought I had flushed those days down that porcelain commode long ago.

I carefully removed the photo without giving any outward sign of emotion. I had discovered as a child with two older sisters that if you do not respond to teasing or harassment, it disappears at a more rapid rate than if you make a fuss and entertain the perpetrators. I took the photo into the District Manager's office and politely laid it on his desk.

"Someone lost this. They left it in my truck by mistake. I thought they might be looking for it," I mentioned nonchalantly.

As I turned to leave, he sighed and sat back in his chair, "I knew you were going to be trouble."

I rolled my eyes, smiled and went back to work, finding it interesting that some man harasses me and I'm the one causing the trouble. The boss considered my mere existence an annoyance.

Shower Power

The Construction and Operating Districts had a few women employees performing clerical duties, however, none in the construction fields until the seventies. The company provided the office women with a small bathroom consisting of a toilet and a sink. The men had a locker room, several showers, toilets, sinks and urinals.

Margaret Thatcher, former Prime Minister of Britain once said, "If you want something said, ask a man. If you want something done, ask a woman." Enter bold Brenda.

When I first reported to the Dells Operating District, I requested a place to store personal items such as feminine hygiene products, an extra sweatshirt and whatnot. I was provided a locker in the warehouse entirely in public view. At times it was embarrassing, but I thought it was the best I could do. When Brenda was transferred to the Dells, they congenially gave her a locker next to mine. The location of the lockers was unacceptable to Brenda. Being a resilient individual and determined to wave the feminist flag, she pointed out the differences in the men's facilities and the women's. I was never certain if it was her fortitude or her beard that intimated management, but within a few weeks construction began and the women at the Dells had their own locker room, shower stalls, two toilets and double sinks beautifully lined with industrial, but attractive tile. The office women loved the new facilities and eagerly moved in.

"Are you happy now?" the disgusted District Manager

asked Brenda.

Brenda stroked her red beard and smirked, "Almost." Brenda was not content until all eight districts had "luxurious" women's restrooms. It took a few years, but it was accomplished. Brenda was a dynamo.

Whomever I Want

When a driver noticed a problem with his company vehicle, a card was filled out requiring the vehicle number, description of the problem, and the driver's name. The card was then dropped in the Garage Repair box. The handwriting of the driver and the inept ability to properly describe the vehicle's situation frequently made it difficult for the Foreman to understand the issue. Fortunately, the mechanics began their shift thirty minutes before the drivers left for the day.

Brenda, our bearded wonder, was working the night shift in the garage during my tour-of-duty at the Dells. I had completed a repair card for the dump truck I had been assigned but evidently I was not clear on the problem. While standing at the gate with several other employees waiting for the infamous whistle to blow signifying the official end of the work day, I heard my name being called.

"Kathy, wait up." I turned to see Brenda, jogging in my direction with her braless pierced boobs swinging to and fro.

"Hey, Brenda. What's up?" I asked, ignoring the grimaces on the faces of my co-workers.

I met Brenda halfway. She had a question about the repair card I had written. I explained the problem, she asked a couple of questions, we discussed it and she said she would get it fixed. I trusted her to do a good job. When Brenda had disappeared around the corner, I was approached by a fiftyish equipment operator outfitted in a stained t-shirt

142

revealing the swollen belly of too many beers.

"You should be careful who you talk to. Someone might think you're like her," he whispered shifting his tarnished lunch pail from one greasy hand to the other.

I was disgusted. I looked at this tobacco-chewing, yellow-toothed smelly old man and wondered if by the same standard I should be seen talking to him.

"I'll talk to whomever I please, thank you," I responded with clinched jaws.

He shrugged, the whistle blew and I marched to my little LUV truck with flowers painted on the side and my head held high.

Mobile Carwash

If I knew I was going to be assigned a water truck I would bring a good book and a stack of magazines - waiting was, generally, the order of the day. But today was one of my lucky assignments and the crew needed lots of water keeping me busy. I was continually washing down the street and spraying water to help with compaction of the ditch as this underground pipeline project was coming to an end. The job was located in a semi-rural area and I made several trips to the nearest fire hydrant nearly a mile away to refill the 5000 gallon tank.

I was traveling on a four lane street returning to the job with a full tank when I stopped for a red light. A burgundy Jaguar convertible carrying two thirty-something men with expensive golf bags stuffed behind the seat pulled next to me in the left lane. The passenger, a dark-haired muscular dude with thick eyebrows sporting golf attire, looked up and realized a woman was driving this big ugly drippy tanker. He made a comment to his sandy-haired mustached buddy and they both laughed. Being used to being gawked at and ridiculed, I smiled my sweetest girly smile.

"Hey," the passenger shouted, "you know how to drive that thing, bitch?"

Bitch? Not that it wasn't one of my unofficial pseudonyms, but it still didn't seem very polite. He didn't even know me.

The sprinklers on the side of the water tanker were three

feet off the ground. So was the side of the Jaguar. So was the face of the impolite man. I smiled sweetly and tapped the control to the sprinkler. Water gently sprayed about two feet from the side of the truck. Not much, but enough.

"No, I'm sorry," I grinned, "I guess I don't know what I'm doing. Want your car washed?"

I fantasized the expensive little testosterone transporter filling up and splashing over the doors as the two stud want-a-bes clambered out of the flood, struggling to save their snooty gaming tools from certain destruction. Then I envisioned my daughter and me not being able to make the house payment after definite job loss. I simply just tapped the control a second time.

The ill-mannered dudes' eyes widen as he realize I had the potential of making a Jacuzzi out of his Jaguar. His mouth dropped, the light turned green and the sports car sped across the intersection leaving me behind. As my tanker slowly chugged along, I smirked. Even though the "gentlemen" waved a special finger in my direction, I won.

Bunk Rat

The old bunk house at the rear of our property in Spokane, Washington, held many mysteries for me. I wondered who had slept here and how long ago. I loved the musty smell, the broken floor, the naked light bulbs dangling by frayed cords from the ceiling and the old bed frames broken and stashed in the corner. Wearing jeans and a Roy Rogers' Rough Rider's hat, I would diligently sweep the dust out the door. It was 1955. I was eight.

After a family trip to a museum at Banff National Park in Canada, I decided to open my own museum. I put up benches for tables, made "watch your step" and "please don't touch" signs, and created displays. I had old bottle caps, a snake skeleton, and some sea shells my sister, Billie, had brought with her from the beach in San Diego. I charged five-cent admission fee. After Mom, Dad, Billie and a neighbor visited the museum; I had a total of fifteen-cents. Billie didn't want to pay to see her own sea shells.

Mom warned me about rats in the old buildings. I never saw any, but I was always sweeping these little black things off the tables and the floor.

Itty Bitty

I opened the driver's door to the boom-truck, tossed my jacket over to the passenger seat, grabbed the side handle and began to climb in.

"Oh, my God!" I screamed as an enormous mother rat hurdled passed me, jumped out the door and scooted under the truck. Her tits were flailing in the breeze as she scampered off.

"Oh crap! Oh no! Oh damn!" I shouted wincing and shuddering from pure creepiness.

I had been dropped off at a substation by a coworker. We were to pick up the boom-truck and deliver it to the main headquarters forty-five miles away. I watched the dust of his pickup as it disappeared over a small hill. He was heading back. It was Thursday, late afternoon and he had a date in a few hours. The official protocol, which my coworker snubbed, was to make certain the vehicle to be transported would start and had plenty of fuel to complete the designated trip. The idea was not to leave an employee stranded miles from home. So much for protocol. I had been hoping to persuade him to drive the truck now that I knew it was rodent ridden.

I hate rats. I don't mind them in cages at a pet store, but not running around the truck I was about to drive. Her milk laden tits triggered more anguish. *Where were the babies?* I looked under the seat, behind the seat and anywhere I thought she might have manufactured a home. I found

147

nothing but a few rags and an old crumpled newspaper. Maybe, I hoped, she was heading toward her nest, not running from it. Maybe, I hoped, her nest was outside the truck.

Fortunately, the truck started easily and had plenty of fuel. My driving attention span was compromised for the first ten miles by rat diversion, but no rodents appeared. I finally relaxed and concentrated on the job at hand – driving in heavy go-home traffic. I arrived at the Fleet Department about two hours past quitting time, so I "pocketed" a little extra overtime dough on my next paycheck. After parking the truck, I re-examined the cab. It was dark, but I didn't see any rodent activity.

The next morning I passed by the "ratty" truck. Harvey, a middle-aged pleasant dayshift mechanic, was about to climb in the cab. He paused and hollered to me.

"Come here. Take a look at this," he grinned.

"What ya got?" I inquired.

"Baby rats. Aren't they cute?"

My boots slid to an abrupt stop. The nightmare returned - the mother rat. Then I remembered the rodent family drama. Mother missing. Babies hungry. Now I felt pity for the poor itty bitties. Sneaking up to the truck, I stood back a few feet and peeked inside. Squirming on the floor were four tiny infant rats about the size of a quarter. Two more babies were dead beneath the seat. I relayed to Harvey the incident with the mother and how I had searched twice for any remaining family members.

"Well, they must have been hiding pretty good," Harvey commented, "I found them curled up in a rag under the seat."

"Guess so," I responded.

Harvey volunteered to dispose of the problem and I didn't ask how. I checked under the seat of every vehicle I drove for the next six months.

Serpentine

When a boy approaches a girl with his hand behind his back, most girls learn quickly that he possesses something icky, sticky or scary. Regrettably, many boys do not outgrow this type of entertainment. Admittedly, I don't like creepy, scaly, slithering creatures which, unfortunately, encourage the juvenile behavior of old-enough-to-know-better adults.

In 1973, while working the night shift in the Auto Repair Shop, I would leave my lavender lunchbox in my personal vehicle until the nine p.m. mealtime. Generally, I would bring a sandwich and a banana or apple and wander over to the break-room in the building across the street. There I would join the janitor, Bill, for some pleasant conversation and a much needed hiatus from the macho mechanics.

One evening after lunch, I made the mistake of leaving my lunchbox at my paltry work station near the tire changing area. When the shift was over, I grabbed my stuff and headed home. As I was departing, I noticed some sideways glances and smirks from my childish coworkers. I shrugged and continued on my way. Arriving home, I placed my lunchbox on the kitchen counter, put on my jammies and crashed into bed.

I am not a squeally girl, nor do I scream. So, the following morning when I opened my lunchbox to discover a dead lizard, I merely gasped, jumped ten-feet back and shuddered. The glances and smirks from the previous evening suddenly made sense. I carefully dumped the carcass in the trash can in the alley and scrubbed the lunchbox with bleach. Upon returning to work that evening, I sauntered into the garage, placed my lunchbox in plain sight and hung my sweatshirt over the handle of the tire jack.

"Any surprises when you got home last night?" one of the mechanics inquired as the rest eavesdropped intently waiting for my reply.

"No. Why?" I answered calm and cool, ignoring the grins.

"Oh, no reason," came the disappointed answer. They all went back to work looking very bewildered.

Fast forward to 1980. I had parked my truck and trailer in The Hole and was heading for the office to fill out my time slip. It had been a hectic week with only one more day to go and I was desperately looking forward to the weekend. A prematurely gray equipment operator with a dark beard and a grimy baseball cap came strolling in my direction. Junior, as he was called, had just parked his vehicle. He was carrying a clipboard and jacket in one hand and the other was hidden behind his back causing suspicion and flashbacks to grade school.

"Hey," he said as he approached, "look what I found." He quickly produced a small garden snake full of life and coiling around his hand. He thrust it within inches of my face. Third grade and Stevie Johnson taught me to remain calm despite my impulse to leap backward quivering in fear.

"Hey, that's cool. You should take it home and put it in your garden," I said nonchalantly while goose bumps crawled up my spine and my stomach convulsed.

Noticeably disappointed with my reaction, Junior agreed and placed the slithering reptile in his lunchbox. Keeping a respectable distance, we walked to the office nonchalantly discussing the boring events of the day.

Energy Speakers

The instructor teaching the public speaking class at the Community College introduced himself and announced, "Since this is the first evening of class, I would like each of you to tell us a little bit about yourself, like where you work or what area you live in, and tell us why you are taking this class. Let's start over here." He pointed to the opposite side of the room.

The first student complied in a monotone voice, "My name's Doug. I am majoring in business and I'm taking this class because my mom thought I should."

The second student spoke in a screechy high voice only dogs could hear, "My name's Annie and I haven't picked a major yet," she proclaimed in her high pitch. I was glad I was sitting on the other side of the room.

Then the next student spoke and so it went until it was my turn. As I was one of the last students to introduce myself, I was nervous and felt uncomfortable. My original plan was to hurry home from the job, shower, change clothes and then rush to class. The job ran late, so I had just barely made it to class on time. I was grimy, filthy, and scruffy. I had washed my face, neck, hands and arms in the women's lavatory before class, but that was all I could manage.

"Hi, I'm Kathy. I work for San Diego Gas and Elec…"

The class didn't give me a chance to finish. They suddenly became a mob. I was shocked. The teacher led the verbal attacks on me, my employer, and the entire utility industry. In the late 1970s the price of electricity was zooming higher every year until, now, in 1980, customers were fuming. I was taken aback by the hostility, harshness and unprofessionalism of the instructor, as well as the students, took me aback. Their questions came quickly and pelted me like a drive-by shooting. *Why is my bill so high? You guys are ripping us off! I have to use candles! The meter readers must be getting a kickback! You all are overpaid! Your company is a cheater and a liar.*

I scrunched down into my seat. I answered all their questions with a weak *"I don't know."* I considered dropping the class. The following day, I approached my supervisor and explained the previous night's situation. I thought, as an employee, I would like to be better prepared to answer questions from customers. He sympathized, as did all employees. Gas crews had rocks thrown at them. Customers would let attack dogs loose on Meter Readers. Electric crews in the back country were threatened with guns. My supervisor referred me to the Public Relations Director, Linda Wilson.

I gave her a call. She set up an appointment for me that afternoon. I expressed my concern about getting to her office on time, because I was working on a construction job in Ramona, over an hour from town by dump truck. She said, "No problem. She would wait for me."

After parking my truck, turning in appropriate paperwork for the job - there's always paperwork - washing the grime off my face, hands and arms, dusting off my jeans, stomping the dirt off my boots, and combing my scruffy hair, I jumped in my little Chevy and drove the thirteen blocks to the Electric Building, the nickname for corporate headquarters. I showed my badge to the security guard and hopped on the elevator to the twelfth floor. It was after five and all the administrative staff had gone for the day. As I searched for her office number, I heard a voice, "You must be Kathy, come in, come in."

She came to the door. The office was huge with a gorgeous view past the maze of tall buildings and out to San Diego Harbor. She smiled and offered her hand. Remembering my dad's words: *A firm handshake reflects a person's character*, I shook hands and smiled, "Nice to meet you. Sorry about my clothes."

She offered me a cup of coffee, "Not to worry."

Linda Wilson was tall, blond, immaculately dressed in a navy-blue skirt, matching sport coat and a pastel pink blouse. A small rose brooch was pinned to her lapel. Her welcoming demeanor chased away any apprehensions I had concerning my attire or my lack of corporate status. Linda, as I was instructed to call her, was an unassuming, non-biased, courteous woman. Instantly, I felt as if we had known one another for years.

"I'm sorry I'm late," I apologized.

"No problem. I had some work I needed to catch up on," she said and motioned for me to sit down.

I explained my experience of the previous evening and how I was embarrassed not to have answers to our customers' concerns. We spent an hour discussing issues involving utilities, the California Public Utilities Commission (CPUC) and the price of oil. In the early 70s, the price of foreign oil had risen over 600% in an extremely short time. The company had layoffs and repositioned employees. The CPUC had passed emergency measures to allow the utilities to pass the cost on to the consumer, much to their chagrin. The problem extended passed the utilities and on to the gas stations. Gas lines were common. The government initiated rules for fueling vehicles to odd and even days depending on the last digit of the license plate.

Towards the end of our conversation Linda paused. She stared at me, cocked her head, and with a slight grin she asked, "Would you be interested in joining the Energy Speaker Corps?"

I hesitated and the look on my face was obvious; I hadn't a clue what she was talking about. She explained how the Corps was just getting started. It consisted of a group of volunteer employees from various areas, departments and positions in the company. The Corps was tasked with educating the public about topics from utility rates, electric and gas safety, energy conservation, career programs, and tours of power plants. I said yes. I was energized.

"You need to get permission from your supervisor as some of the training programs will take you away from your regular work."

I told Linda I would get back with her after I discussed it with my boss. I thanked her for her time and closed the door on the way out. Like an excited little girl, I skipped down the hall to the elevator.

Arriving at a pivotal point in my career, I wanted to be a part of the corporation, not just a number. I needed a time of discovery and this was it. Now, if only my supervisor would give me approval.

When I asked if I could join the Energy Speaker Corps, my boss paused and told me he would contact Linda Wilson to confirm. The following day he gave me the okay. Women's Lib was at full throttle and I think he was afraid to say no.

It wasn't as easy as I thought to become a member of the Energy Speaker Corps. There were classes on verbal communication, giving an effective presentation, and using visual aids. Since I was currently enrolled in the public speaking class, I had an advantage over some of the other employees.

After attending several sessions, a decision was made and the Corps was handpicked. If you were one of the "chosen few" you received a "Western Union Mailgram" from the president of the company:

CONGRATULATIONS YOU HAVE BEEN SELECTED TO JOIN SDG&E'S PRESTIGIOUS ENERGY SPEAKERS CORPS. IN HONOR OF THE OCCASION, YOU AND YOURSPOUSE, OR FRIEND, ARE INVITED TO DINE WITH MY WIFE AND I AND THE ENERGY SPEAKERS ON WEDNESDAY, NOVEMBER 5 AT 7:00 P.M. IN THE

WESTGATE HOTEL'S EMBASSY ROOM...

SINCERELY,
R.E.MORRIS

I was in. It was a great networking dinner. I met employees from departments I didn't even know existed. The Energy Speakers provided encouragement, awareness and enthusiasm to otherwise, sometimes, very boring jobs.

Always Learning

The Energy Speaker Corps involved a lot of training and informative sessions. Most of the meetings revolved around the ever rising utility rates. I listened intently. Some of the reasons offered seemed logical and others did not, but I was not in a position to question corporate suits sporting power ties.

We were encouraged to accept assignments based on the time available from our regular jobs in our individual departments. Most of us made presentations once or twice a month. It was 1981 and I was still working in construction. I tried to make my commitments late afternoon, evenings or weekends to avoid conniving dispatchers who would send me to another hemisphere to make certain I would be late for a presentation and make me look incompetent. I turned down invitations during my regular work hours and other, more "flexible" speakers would come to the rescue.

For our first few presentations, we were encouraged to partner with another member of the Corps. It took the pressure off and made you feel comfortable knowing you had backup. The first presentation I was assigned solo was for a church group; the subject, energy conservation. I felt comfortable with that topic. Then I was assigned several presentations on rising utility rates and was given updated information. Each time the groups were hostile. No matter how I presented the information, I was questioned and accused of cheating the innocent public out of their precious hard-earned money. I was afraid the public was right…at least, part of the time. Not feeling comfortable with those questionable corporate issues, I pretended to be "busy." My future presentations centered on electric safety, conservation, career programs and non-traditional jobs.

When I was asked to give a talk about non-traditional jobs, it was frequently to a women's group. The first few talks I gave seemed empty. I had no visual aids, no photos, and no good examples. All the other corporate presentations had slideshows, posters, handouts or other items to enhance audience awareness. For the non-traditional presentation, I decided to create my own slideshow.

With camera in hand, I scheduled my visits with other women employees based on our combined work schedules. If I was assigned to a job near a facility where I knew a woman worked, I would contact her first. Then I would drop by, take a few photos, jot down some notes and be on my way. The women were excited and eager to assist.

Kurt, the company photographer, was intrigued by my project and offered to help. Together we coordinated photo shoots and interviews. With Kurt's help, it took only six weeks to complete. When the slideshow was finished, I presented it to the Energy Speakers with mixed reviews. A few of the power-tie oriented thought it was a waste of time, but the rest thought it created good karma for the company. The latter group included the company CEO. I was in.

I had given my "Women in Non-Traditional Jobs" presentation with my new slideshow several times when I was invited to an elementary school in an area of town dominated by Hispanic and African-American citizens. The group consisted of the fifth and sixth grade classes, all 235 of them, both boys and girls. The substance of the presentation was to introduce possible careers choices to these young people. My non-traditional presentation was the only career program SDG&E had at the time. I explained to the school principal how my program depicted only women in various careers. She believed it would be acceptable as long as I explained to the children how the jobs were open to both men and women. I eagerly agreed.

I reported to the office and was escorted by an eager Vice Principal to the auditorium. The event was enjoyable for me and my audience. The kids sat, imagining driving an eighteen-wheeler. They pretended to use a clutch with their left foot and shift gears with their right hand. I explained the duties of various occupations like chemist, electrician and meter reader. I asked them questions and helped with the answers. When I completed the presentation and the children were heading back to class, two of the teachers stopped to thank me.

"Let me shake your hand," grinned a Hispanic teacher and grabbed my hand with enthusiasm.

"This was wonderful," said an African-American woman.

"Thank you," I replied, "It was fun."

"I don't think you understand," they responded, almost in unison.

The two women explained that I had more than met their

expectations. I had shown women of various ethnic backgrounds as electricians, chemists, meter readers, meter repair and engineers. I was puzzled.

"I tried to show women in all types of work environments," I said.

"Yes, you did."

I shrugged, "So... did I do something right?"

The two smiling women explained. It seemed as if the children in these neighborhoods had limited expectations. These children thought they could only perform entry level positions with no hope of moving up.

"I showed women in entry level positions," I reminded them, still puzzled.

"Yes," the Hispanic teacher smiled, "but the women were of all ethnicities and you explained how they could get promotions and expand their careers and move up that ladder."

The women each gave me a sincere hug, asked for my card, and said they wanted to invite me back again. For me it was an epiphany. The entire time I was creating the program, I was thinking "women." I was not thinking "race" or "culture." My goal was to encourage young people – all young people – to follow their dreams and not limit themselves. Over the next few weeks, I added more photos to my project. I created a second presentation portraying a more general career program to be offered to both girls and boys. I made certain I had individuals of both sexes and all ethnic backgrounds in each type of career. My goal was to open up a world of possibilities to children of all backgrounds.

For the next eighteen years, I was a guest speaker for Lyons Clubs, Kiwanis, schools, church groups and numerous other community groups and organizations. My cartoon book, "My Mom, the Truck Driver" had been out for several years and because of my non-traditional occupations, I became the company's representative for Women's Opportunity Week, Women's History Month and many other career and encouragement programs. I was invited to speak at the San Diego Women's Conference and television and radio interviews. I loved every minute of it.

I began writing a monthly safety and conservation column in a newsletter for an international non-profit at the request of one of their employees. In the, now-retired *East County News*, I wrote a column called *East County Women*. I interviewed the woman and emphasized their role in the community. Through the Energy Speaker Corps, I met employees from various occupations and departments within the company. These acquaintances, ultimately, unbolted corporate doors.

Don't Look That Smart

When my daughter was two-years-old, I decided to attend San Diego City College. It was the fall of 1967.

The registration process included a math assessment examination. I eagerly took all the required tests. A few weeks later I received the test scores in the mail. The next step was to choose the classes I wanted and was qualified for, then go to the community college gym and stand in line to get approval. When it was finally my turn, I showed the counselor my chosen classes.

"You can't take this math class," he grumbled shoving the list across the table.

I was confused. "But I thought I could if my assessment score was high enough?"

"Let me see that." The counselor grabbed the test score card from my hand. "Are you Kathleen?"

I confirmed I was. He frowned and looked me up and down several times. I was dressed in my favorite surfer sundress and custom sandals made by the famous Ocean Beach sandal maker. My bleached-blond hair was straight and parted in the middle.

"You sure don't look that smart," he grumbled, begrudgingly signing my card and shoving it back to me.

I aced that math class.

No Backing Up

I drove the dump truck full of gravel down the narrow residential road to the job site. The job involved the installation of a gas line along the edge of the road. I parked and waited for instructions from the foreman, Kenny, a friendly fortyish family man who had the habit of always bragging about his son's baseball team. It was late afternoon and so far this had been an uneventful day. I had been assigned this job for a little over a week. The crew was good and we all worked well together.

After several minutes, Kenny motioned for me to bring the load of gravel. As I approached, he hopped on the side step and instructed me to pull across the road and back up to the ditch. Kenny motioned for a couple of laborers to stop traffic while I positioned the truck. I drove across the road blocking traffic, facing a small white picket fence embellishing a craftsmen-style fifties-era home. My left foot disengaged the clutch pedal. I checked my mirrors, reached for the gearshift lever and began to put the truck in reverse.

SNAP! The lever broke off in my hand. The truck was still in forward gear. If I lifted my foot from the clutch, the truck, with me in it, and twelve yards of gravel would plunge through the cute little fence and into the sweet little house. I looked in the mirror and saw bewildered Kenny, motioning for me to back up and dump the load. The noise of the diesel engine drowned out my shouts for help. In desperation, I grabbed the shift lever and waved it out the window. Kenny looked perplexed. Abruptly the realization of the situation set in. His mouth dropped open and the whites of his eyes made him look like a surprised Disney character. He rushed to the truck.

"What happened!?" he shouted.

"I don't know. It broke off. I'm in gear!" My leg was shaking from the strain as I continued pressing on the clutch.

After a few justifiably cursing remarks, Kenny ran to the loader operator to explain the situation. I pulled on the emergency brake and I sat with both feet on the clutch pedal as the laborers allowed the frustrated traffic to pass while a solution was being found. Mercifully, the road was not heavily traveled.

Jose, our welder, opened the passenger door and asked what the problem was. I showed him the broken gearshift. He hopped up on the step to get a better look.

"I'll be back," Jose said and I assured him that I was not going anywhere. In a moment he returned with a couple of pieces of pipe. "Try this," he said as he handed me one.

When the shift lever broke it left a small piece of metal protruding from the floorboard about two inches long. The first pipe Jose handed me was too big. He quickly handed me the other pipe. It fit loosely, but better. With the assistance of the pipe, I was able to move the shift lever, or what was left of it, into the neutral position. I could take my foot off the clutch. My leg burned.

Still blocking the road and still full of gravel, the second part of the plan was to pull the truck back to the edge of the ditch with the loader. A chain was attached to the rear, a couple of tugs and I was lined up to dump the load. I raised the dump bed; the gravel spilled out and I lowered the bed. The third part of the plan was to get the ailing beastly truck out of the street and let the project continue. Jose removed the tow chain from the rear of the dump truck and repositioned it in the front. The loader operator then pulled me and my villainous truck to the side of the road. Kenny called the office and a mechanic was dispatched. The mechanic arrived in about twenty minutes, inspected the problem and called a tow truck. He waited patiently for its arrival while collecting overtime.

As Jose gave me a ride back to the district office, I waved a fond farewell to the pathetic piece of metal.

Don't Mind the Space Suit, Ma'am

Every generation leaves in its wake rubbish for the following generation to clean up. PCB was one of the piles of doo doo left from the "atomic" age. PCB (polychlorinated biphenyl) was a coolant added to the oil contained in capacitors and transformers – those big gray cans hanging from electric poles or those big green boxes on street corners. PCB was proven to be a toxic and persistent organic pollutant and carcinogenic (cancer causing) agent. It needed to be disposed of. Being the first to go were the obvious culprits, the transformers leaking oil.

When one of our Electric Troublemen spied one of the evil leaky containers he would fill out a form. The form would then be handed to his superior who would make a copy and send it to the Fleet office. The Fleet office would make a copy and hand it to the Hazardous Materials office who would make a copy and hand it to the HazMat foreman and another tree would die in vain.

For some unknown reason, I found the field of hazardous materials interesting. I bothered the HazMat foreman with so many questions that he asked if I would like to attend a HazMat class. I was eager. The class was training for becoming a member of the prestigious cleanup crew. I wasn't fully aware of consequences of that part of the equation, but I was up for the challenge.

When a Toubleman reported that a transformer was actually leaking onto the ground, it became an urgent situation. The cleanup crew was on twenty-four-hour duty. We would take turns being on the call-out list.

One pleasant summer morning, we received a report that there was a leaking transformer in the prestigious community of Coronado. We gathered our tools, HazMat suits, gloves and facemasks, climbed in the truck and headed toward the felonious transformer. If the leaking oil was in the vicinity of potential foot traffic, the Troubleman would set up traffic cones and keep watch until we reached the site. This was the situation in Coronado.

The procedure upon arrival at the scene of the crime was to position the vehicle next the pole, put on our HazMat suits, gloves, and face masks. Everything was disposable. The suits were white woven paper-like fabric. The facemasks were white. The rubber gloves were white. The ensemble made us look like astronauts on a moonwalk.

It was easy to imagine how a resident would feel when they looked out their living room window and saw trucks with flashing lights, traffic cones, and a bunch of people dressed in protective clothing looking like a spacewalk. We were just putting on our suits when an elderly woman stormed from her house and demanded to know what we were doing. I was the closest to respond and since I had not walked in the offending area, I could approach her.

"Good morning," I said in a friendly, but professional voice.

"What's all this?" she grumbled. She was not friendly or professional, but must have been rich or she wouldn't have been living in Coronado.

I explained that we were just going to clean up a little oil spill and change out the transformer on the pole. She need not worry. We would be out of her way in a couple of hours. My explanation did not pacify her. The rest of the crew had begun the cleanup process and an electric crew had arrived with a bucket truck to begin replacing the leaky transformer with a non-PCB safe one. This activity made the lady even more annoyed. It was then I discovered that my rich little old lady had the vocabulary of a gutter mudder. She stormed back to her house and protested, "I'll see about this!" I apologized for the inconvenience and joined the crew.

My foreman, who did not like talking to unhappy customers, was glad I had taken on the task. But, when he noticed it was not going well, he radioed his supervisor, who, in turn, called his boss in Corporate Headquarters. Before long the job was cluttered with suits and ties.

The company had been removing and cleaning up PCB transformers for several months. The local news media had just found out about the hazardous oil and, since bad news sells, needed something to get their audience stirred up and improve ratings. They chose Coronado. Had the leaky transformer been in an impoverished area, no one would have cared.

The photographers and reporters arrived shortly after the suits. The utility rates were increasing and customers were angry at SDG&E. I discovered my lady friend took advantage of the situation and had called to report dangerous activity in front of her house. Cameras and microphones were abundant. We kept referring them to the corporate attendees.

I have often wondered about the intelligence of a news cameraman. It doesn't seem smart to ignore security cones and follow someone around who is wearing protective clothing and special boots. Especially when the cameraman is walking through the same stuff that is being cleaned up and carefully deposited in a large black barrel marked with one of the scary numbered diamonds with all kinds of warnings printed all over it. But, I guess (I hope) they are well paid.

We continued our cleanup, ignoring the cameras and reporters, put the leaking transformer in a HazMat barrel, took off our disposable suits and accessories, put them in the barrel, loaded it on the truck, picked up all our tools and went back to the headquarters. At the office, we made eight copies of our report: one for the HazMat Department records, one for the Fleet office, one for the Troubleman, one for his superior, and one for the city, county, state and federal governments and another tree would die in vain.

We all rushed home to see our television début. But, cleaning up spilled oil would have to wait until some other day. We were preempted by a four car crash on Highway 5.

HazMat Nate

Nate refused to speak to me. He never made eye contact and tried not to remain in the same room. Nate was a short stocky dark-haired man with a stern and forceful voice. I kept out of his way and the dispatchers made certain we did not work together on the same jobs. That was until there was a HazMat delivery to a site near Solvang, California, about 260 miles north of San Diego.

There were four of us assigned to the trip. Four drivers and four trucks, pulling forty-foot trailers full of fifty-five gallon drums filled with PCB (polychlorinated biphenyl) and who-knows-what other creepy, hazardous, icky stuff. The barrels were adorned with diamond-shaped decals labeled with numbers indicating the harmful contents. There were only a handful of drivers trained to transport and clean up these hazardous materials. Nate, Ken, Robbie and I were among the chosen few.

Ken was senior and in charge of the trip. It was early March and the weather was fickle. Ken had suggested we get an early start leaving about 4:00 AM to avoid traffic and the predicted bad weather. This created controversy amongst our troop as we would not get paid for the early start since it was our choice. Nate did not speak. Robbie was the dissenting vote. He ultimately gave in when we agreed to buy him breakfast at our first stop. Our only communications between trucks were short-wave radios. We tested them before leaving.

Kathleen McLaughlin

We each had the proper paperwork to show the Highway Patrol (there's always paperwork) and our trucks and trailers passed through the weigh stations without incident. We stopped for breakfast at a small café just off the freeway with plenty of space to park four trucks and trailers. Robbie paid for his own meal, admitting that it had been a good idea to start early. During breakfast Nate still did not speak, except to ask the waitress for another cup of coffee.

Ten hours after we had left San Diego, we arrived at the hazardous waste dump. It only sprinkled on us going through Los Angeles and the traffic had been light - by LA standards. The dump site was in a remote canyon with warning signs stating health risks lining the road leading up to the main gate. Ken gathered up the paperwork and stiffly limped to the office. Hours behind the wheel had taken its toll on all of us. With our papers in order, we were instructed to a specific area where each barrel had to be unloaded with a forklift. We positioned the barrels by wiggling them to the edge of the trailer so the lift operator could reach them. The barrels were heavy, some weighing more than two-hundred pounds. The lift operator was concerned.

"We need to get our asses in gear. I need to get off on time today," he smirked. I guess he wanted someone to ask him why, but no one obliged. With a sleazy wink, he added, "I got plans tonight. You know what I mean."

I forced a smile. Ken shook his head in disgust. Robbie and Nate just ignored him. We were also concerned about finishing as we had not indulged in a regular meal since breakfast and had only grabbed a snack from a vending machine at one of the truck scales.

We developed an unloading routine. Nate and Robbie would wiggle them to Ken and I who would then position them for the lift operator. It was smooth and deliberate as if it had been choreographed. I caught a glimpse of Nate smiling. I wondered if he was mocking me. I ignored him and worked hard, as usual. The barrels were dirty and grimy. We all looked as if we had been dragged through the mud by the time we had finished. Ken completed the paperwork and being the only one, who had previously made this trip, instructed us to follow him to the hotel. He had made reservations at a place a few miles away with a side street that would accommodate our trucks and trailers.

Ken checked us in at the registration desk and there was some brief grumblings about how I was costing the company money because two men could share a room and I had to have my own. Ken handed out the keys. He and Robbie shared a room and Nate was the lucky one to be assigned to a single. My room was small, but comfortable. I quickly showered and put on some clean jeans, a pink t-shirt and color coordinating socks and bandana. The restaurant across the street was the agreed dinning venue. I was hungry. Evidently, so was everyone else, because there had been no time wasted in getting scrubbed up and meeting for dinner.

We started with a cold beer. The dirt, dust and mud of the day needed to be washed from our throats and since we were not going to be driving any more it was permissible.

Throughout the evening meal, Nate was silent with only a couple of mumbling comments to Ken. By now I had gotten over his rejection and he had become invisible. After dinner, Nate went back to his room and Robbie, Ken and I decided to wander down the street to a small pub. We told jokes, stories and grumbled about upper management. I drank another beer - two being my absolute limit - and walked back to the hotel. Ken and Robbie stayed for another nightcap.

The following morning, I packed my things, checked out of my room, placed my bag in the truck and met the others for breakfast. Ken and Robbie were late. As I approached the restaurant, I saw Nate reading the morning paper through the plastic in the stand.

"Good morning," I said feeling a little rebellious.

"Good morning," Nate replied.

I rocked back on my heels and tried not to lose my balance. I had not heard his voice more than a dozen times over six years and had never heard it directed at me. My head tilted sideways like a puzzled puppy. There was a long pause.

"You know," he began, "I never thought you pulled your weight. I always thought that everyone else had to work harder to make up for you. I was wrong."

I was flabbergasted. I swallowed hard.

"Yesterday, you worked your little fanny off," he finished with a grin, "You did your part. I apologize."

"Thank you," I said bewildered. Maybe, I thought, Nate was not so bad after all.

Ken and Robbie joined us. Ken raised his eyebrows when he saw Nate and me standing next to one another. We grabbed a table for breakfast and began discussing the trip home.

"Pass the salt, please," asked Nate.

"Sure," I said and handed him both the salt and the pepper.

"Thanks."

This exchange of dialog caused wide eyes and sideways glances from the other two.

It took two hours longer returning to San Diego. We encountered heavy rains and winds all the way home. The tension of driving in bad weather is grueling. By the time I picked up my daughter from her grandma's and reached home I was pooped.

The next morning, as I arrived to work I passed Nate in the hall. He nodded with a slight grin and I responded in kind. For the next twenty years he became an ally.

Eventually, we both were promoted to administrative positions and he even stopped in my office to say 'hello' and bought me a soda on a hot day.

Rung One

The company decided the Miramar Yard Foreman, Floyd, was overworked. He was responsible for the receiving, storage and delivery of all the large material, including transformers, poles, reels of cable, cross arms, gas pipe and a huge list of other items. Plus, he was expected to field jobs before the poles were to be delivered to job sites. Poor Floyd.

With the population of San Diego growing between 1975 and 1980 at a faster rate than any other city in the United States, SDG&E had to scurry to keep up with the needs of the expanding customer base. This growth pattern funneled into the early 80's and kept us all hustling. New housing developments were bouncing up all over, creating a backlog at Miramar Yard. Enter the newly created position of *Material Distribution Foreman.*

When the job bid appeared on the bulletin board, I instantly snatched it and made a copy. This was my chance to creep up on that illusive corporate ladder. I had completed more than half of the college supervision classes and was a member of the Energy Speaker Corps. I wanted to be a bigger part of the corporation and it wasn't going to break my heart to get out of the union. I sent in my application. Weeks passed. I had given up. Then at the end of a difficult and dirty day, I received a note from the dispatcher.

"Report to the Miramar offices for an interview tomorrow at 11:30 AM" he griped. This upset him as he then had to arrange my workload around the interview.

The next morning he snarled and assigned me to washing cars and delivering paperwork (there is always paperwork) to other offices within the four-block area. Miramar was fifteen miles north of downtown San Diego and with traffic concerns I asked to leave at ten o'clock. The dispatcher, deciding that it was in his best interest not to be the reason I was late, sneered an *"okay."* He believed it was a bit early, but I mentioned that I thought a change of clothes was in order. He was hoping I would attend the interview wearing dirty jeans and a soiled t-shirt.

A fashion show had taken place in my living room the previous evening as I walked the runway between the couch and the chair exhibiting several options to my limited audience of Karen and the neighbor, Stephanie. A unanimous decision voted for the navy blue skirt and jacket with a pastel yellow blouse. At work, I scurried to my car to retrieve my business apparel and into the women's restroom and made the quick change. I had brought two pairs of pantie hose in case of the inevitable run. I was glad. I tossed my "work clothes" in my car, jumped in the company vehicle and nerve-rackingly drove to Miramar.

My interview was with the Material Distribution Supervisor, Geoff Simon and his boss, Material Distribution Manager, Roger Waddell. I arrived eighteen minutes early and was instructed to wait. The Administrative Assistant, Judi, smiled, offered me a cup of coffee and gave a sincere *"good luck."* I had met uncanny Geoff during my many trips to Miramar hauling material, but I had never met Roger. In a few minutes, a man exited the manager's office, closed the door and glared at me and Judi. Judi shrugged and gave me a puzzled look. "Another applicant," she said.

In a few minutes the door reopened and I was invited in by Geoff, a slightly built man with a large head. Roger Waddell introduced himself without making eye contact and motioned me to sit. Dressed in a sport jacket and tie he reminded me of a corporate Humpty Dumpty with a round body and skinny legs. They asked me basic questions about deliveries to the districts, gave me irrational hypothetical situations, asking me how I would handle the problems and asked if I had any questions about the job. I really didn't, since the position had never existed before, but took the opportunity to mention my involvement with the Energy Speaker Corps and my supervision college classes. They were not impressed. The interview lasted less than ten minutes. They superficially thanked me for my interest and I was dismissed. As I was leaving, Judi issued another "good luck."

I heard nothing for two and a half weeks - then the news. I got the job! My friends outside the company were ecstatic and helped me celebrate with a barbeque. But employees gave me mixed reviews. A few of my supporters gave me big "attagirls." The non-supporters came to the conclusion that I had been awarded the job because I was a woman. They could not comprehend that maybe my experience, my college education and my knowledge had anything to do with it. I never knew the truth, but I was determined to excel at the position.

Zack, one of my competitors for the job was now my subordinate. I took special care in tiptoeing around him and giving him the jobs I had been told he most enjoyed. He carefully watched my progress for the first year.

"Ya know…I was pissed when you got the job," Zack finally admitted.

"I know," I responded sympathetically.

"Now, I'm glad I didn't get it," he grinned. Zack confessed he didn't realize how much paperwork was involved and how difficult it was to deal with cantankerous district supervisors.

The latter was, in fact, the most demanding.

Hear Me Roar… Quietly

"You'd better get over here, now!" Judi whispered into the phone.

"Why?"

"They're having a meeting and, I think, they 'conveniently' forgot to invite you."

I had been in the new position of Material Distribution Foreman at Miramar Yard for nearly two weeks. Judi, the Manager's Administrative Assistant, was my biggest supporter. She had worked at the Distribution Warehouse and Storage Yard for four years. Judi was a petite, quiet, intelligent, efficient and very unassuming young woman. She became my "informant."

I thanked Judi, picked up my notepad and hurried across the yard to the main conference room several acres away. The Yard Foreman, Floyd, with whom I shared the office, had left a few minutes earlier carrying a clipboard. I wondered where he had gone, but didn't think much of it at the time. Entering the building, I sprinted up the stairs, and hesitated for a moment to regain my composure before entering the conference room. The meeting was supposed to start at 10 AM, it was 9:59. Judi got me there just in time.

The conference room was typical. The corporate headquarters received all the good stuff and the outlying districts received all the hand-me-downs. A scratched center table with missed-matched chairs dominated the room with a white board at one end and a coffee maker and donuts at the other. There were about fifteen foreman and supervisors from the outlying district warehouses. Some were dressed in suits, some in sport shirts, and some in jeans and work shirts. When I opened the door and entered, they were telling dirty jokes, helping themselves to coffee, complaining about not having their favorite donut available and choosing where to sit. As I entered, some turned away, some grimaced, some smiled, some introduced themselves and one shook my hand with extreme superficial enthusiasm. I smiled, and made a mental note to keep him at a distance and my back to the wall.

The Manager, Roger, who was in retirement mode, gave me a puzzled stare. He made no reference to the fact that I had been left off the memo distribution list and neither did I. The rest of the attendees, I'm confident, were oblivious.

"I'm sure you have not met our newest member to the Material Control Department? I would like you to meet…ah…Kathy…she's our new Material Distribution Foreman," Roger said rolling his eyes.

The other gentlemen nodded. The ones who were not gentlemen looked away or began writing on their notepads.

"Oh, Kathy, would you mind taking notes?" Roger smirked. All eyeballs, showing white, turned to the manager, then to me wondering if the women's libber samurai was going to jump out and wave her sword.

"Certainly," I smiled sweetly, "not a problem." I paused and looked around at the group. "Who normally takes notes?"

One of the members mumbled something about how he didn't think anybody did but was interrupted. "I'll do it," Mathew, a self-confident fortyish man volunteered. He smiled at me compassionately. I knew he was one I could trust.

The Menial Meeting

"She's doing very well in math and science," said Mr. Teacher. Mom and Dad smiled. I cringed waiting the inevitable qualifying remark. "For a girl," Mr. Teacher added. My parents were a few generations ahead of their time in their unbiased thought processes.

"Didn't you say she is getting all A's?" Dad asked rhetorically, "Aren't all A's the same? Boy or Girl?"

"Yes, she's doing very well."

"For a girl," Mom clarified.

Mr. Teacher smiled condescendingly and moved on to talk to other, not as contrary, parents. Dad put his arm around my shoulder and squeezed a little. Mom smiled and winked. We moved on to examine my school projects on display at the semester Open House at Collier Junior High School. It was the early 60's and girls were expected to do well in chorus, but not math; homemaking, but not science.

Later that semester the English department conducted a three-week career program. We took surveys and answered questions revealing our interests and desires. At the end of the first week we received the results of our individual surveys in the form of a list of potential careers based on our current skills and passions. I ranked high in engineering careers – there's that math and science again – and low in domestic – which was no surprise to anyone especially my homemaking teacher. She was always making me sit at a "breadboard." Having to use a breadboard for a "desk" instead of being able to join the other girls at a table was the ultimate humiliation. I was used to it.

My eyes slowing fell down the list of professions that had been designated appropriate for me; automotive engineer, mechanic, counselor, museum curator, architect, doctor, lawyer, corporate chief – *Wait! Back up! Architect? I would love to be an architect!* I was thrilled. I loved buildings, houses, structures. When I was nine I had read an article on Frank Lloyd Wright's Fallingwater house in Pennsylvania. I wanted to be just like Frank and design buildings, structures, and create floor plans. My father was a painting contractor and during the summer months I was permitted to accompany him to job sites. I confirmed measurements, project estimates and help with the calculations. So, when I saw "architect" on the list of potential careers, I was elated.

The next step in the career program assignment was to conduct an interview with someone in our selected career or profession and share the results with the class. Dad arranged an interview with Mr. P, an architect Dad had worked with on several occasions. He thought Mr. P would be a good candidate for my interview and would give me encouraging advice.

On the appointed day, I dressed in my best, most business-like attire and Mom chauffeured me to the architect's office, located on prestigious Shelter Island boarding San Diego Harbor. With pen in one hand and a list of questions in the other, I eagerly entered the office. This was my first introduction to the arrogance and conceit of the don't-bother-me-kid executives. I would run across his type many times later in life and I would acquire the ability to deal with them. But this was my first and I was very apprehensive. He answered all my questions, checking his watch every couple of minutes, and impatiently waited for me to write down the answers. I was a little slow as I had not taken the shorthand class recommended for girls. When we concluded, I thanked him for his time and he dutifully showed me the door. As I was leaving, he smiled and made the gut-wrenching statement that would alter my life.

By the time I reached the car, tears filled my eyes. Mom smiled at me, then saw the tears and quickly asked what was wrong. I sat for several minutes staring out the windshield seeing nothing.

"Mommy… he said…he said that girls don't make good architects."

Mom patted my hand and we drove home in silence. Mom teared up, too. The following day Dad had a serious talk with Mr. P.

Architect Revival

The architect in me who had been sleeping for over thirty-seven years awoke one morning in the fall of 1983. This uneducated, ill-informed and unaware architect (aka me) decided to design and build my own house. I had subscribed to *Architectural Digest* and spent many a Sunday touring "Open Houses" persuading the real estate agent that I might be a prospective buyer. But all the time I was looking at the structure, floor plan and general layout of the home, deciding what I liked, didn't like or "not on your life."

After seeing an article about some pretentious persnickety over-the-hill Hollywood star and his loft home, I decide I wanted a loft, too. I also wanted a view, big garage, lots of windows, a separate laundry room and space for my horse. I picked up my pencil; the drafting tools left to me by my late father and started drawing away. After several months of thinking, drawing and more thinking, it was mentioned to me by John - my new beau - that I might want to buy the property first. I began shopping.

The closer to town; the more expensive the lot. I began looking east toward the foothills of San Diego County. In Jamul, I found a lot on a hill, sort of a land-locked peninsula. It was February, 1984, and the sky was clear. The view was an incredible 300 degrees. To the west I could see twenty miles to the Pacific Ocean and Coronado Bridge. A slight turn to the south and I could see the Coronado Islands in Mexico. Turn a little more and beautiful hills, valleys and mountains. The owner of the lot lived nearby and had just finished building his own home. He promised to assist in dealing with the permits, easements and other legislative hurdles. I was hooked. I brought John and a couple of friends to see the lot. They were as amazed as I was. Now, I needed to sell my little house in La Mesa.

Since I was determined not to pay someone for something I thought I could do, I decided to sell the house myself. I posted signs and advertised in the papers. I was approached by several real estate agents, but smilingly refused their services until Mike appeared. Mike was a fireman for the City of La Mesa. Their shifts were twenty-four on and twenty-four off. Mike had a real estate license and sold property between putting out fires and saving lives. I liked Mike. He was direct, understanding and he promised to charge me only for the services rendered. When I had a buyer interested, I had several phone conversations with Mike. The buyer and I settled on a price. Mike assisted with the paperwork (there's always paperwork) and my cute little house was sold.

Now, finally, I could buy the lot in Jamul. Now, finally, I could build the house of my dreams. Now, finally, I came to the realization I had nowhere to live in the interim. I thought about renting an apartment, but most would not accept pets and I wasn't going to give up Lillian. The new Jamul neighbor suggested I live in a trailer on the property while the house was being built. With Karen in her own apartment and my first grandchild on the way, it sounded like a great idea. I could have Lillian with no problem and I could monitor the progress of the job. I shopped for a trailer that could "temporarily" house me and the dog. By the time escrow closed, I had found a twenty-four-foot travel trailer. It was perfect. I told Mike my plan. He informed me of county laws restricting me from moving the trailer to the property until the water and septic systems were installed. I had to go to plan B or maybe C or D, unfortunately, I didn't have any of those plans yet.

Finding a place for the trailer was an unforeseen challenge. Mobile home parks did not rent temporary trailers spaces. Some vacation-type trailer parks did not rent for more than two weeks. I finally discovered a place that would take me for a few months. I hoped it would be for one month. It turned out to be three.

A grading plan had to be approved by the County of San Diego. I decided to draw my own grading plan. A topographical map of the property, purchased for a pittance, and some free brochures available at the county engineering department blazed the trail through the brush to my first "official" drawings. My neighbor in La Mesa worked for the city engineering department and managed to help with the numerous corrections to my novice drawings. They were finally approved and grading could begin.

A friend of a friend knew a guy with a small bulldozer who could do the work. It took three times as long and cost three times as much. I thought about trashing the project. A decision to redesign the house to fit the property instead of making the property fit the house would have been a much better - and cheaper - idea. Tearful nights and several scribbled spreadsheets later I decided to push on. No friends or friends of friends would be hired in the future.

After the husband of the woman who worked at the Jamul Post Office finished installing the septic system and the leech lines (they weren't really friends, so my new rules didn't count), and stage one of the electrical was installed, I was ready to move the trailer onto the property. The move was mercifully uneventful and I settled in.

While living in the trailer park, I was allowed to hook up to their utilities. Hot water was plentiful and they had cable TV. After moving my temporary home to my lot in the boonies, I became disturbingly aware of my requirement for amenities. The surrounding hills interfered with TV reception. I could only get two stations; one was a network and the other was from Mexico. I took the opportunity to brush up on my minimal Spanish. The trailer had a small inefficient water heater. Southern Californians have been encouraged for years to take water-saving five-minute showers. I pride myself in my ability to accomplish this feat. But the trailer took things to a new level. It only held three, maybe four minutes worth of hot water. Many times I would be all soaped up only to be tortured by freezing cold liquid. I tried washing my hair in the sink. My personal hygiene habits took a horrific plunge. I began showering at work at the end of the day. There was a small shower in the women's restroom. This triggered issues as I was required to become organized at 5 AM and actually think about what I was going to need at 3 PM. I would repeatedly forget to bring a towel or a change of clothes or shampoo or some other basic need. Sometimes I would stop by the Jamul hair salon and get a quick shampoo and leave wet. The stylist was very accommodating and would squeeze me in between appointments.

Convinced that I could be my own general contractor, my first step was to hire a draftsman to draw up the official plans then get the plans approved by the county. With the sensational view, I wanted lots and lots of windows. This created some energy calculation anxieties for the draftsman. The windows had to be double-paned which was a fairly new concept, but being eco-friendly, I was all for it. In addition, a minimum number of square footage of floor space had to be tiled. I was able to meet the requirements. I would have loved to have built an entirely energy independent home, but that was not within my paltry budget.

I sent the plans out for bid for plumbing, foundation and framing. The plumber was the nephew of a coworker and did an outstanding job. To save money, I was his laborer and with John's help, dug the trenches for the sewer and water service which had to be completed before the foundation could be installed.

The foundation was poured on the world's hottest day. The team started the process at 7 AM. A crew member stayed late into the evening to spray water over the cement so it wouldn't dry too fast. The frame was erected in an incredibly short time. I was packing my bags and mentally decorating the living room. Then the clock stopped. The electrical wiring, the plumbing, heating and cooling system, the solar water heater and insulation took an eternity. I unpacked my bags and resolved to living in the trailer for the rest of my life.

Being my own general contractor was the biggest hurdle in the progression. I had no idea the order of things. I wasn't sure how long each stage would take. So, I didn't know when to schedule the next step. Sometimes several weeks would drag by before the next phase would even be started. I couldn't expect the subcontractors to impede another customer's project just because I didn't know how to schedule mine. I had learned in the corporate world that grandma was right, *"you catch more flies with honey than with vinegar."* You can't annoy someone when you desperately need them. So I smiled with my bottom teeth and played the sweet-lady card. The subcontractors were nice and assisted me with other issues, offering advice and encouragement. They also allowed me to use their contractor's license numbers to buy supplies and materials wholesale. It probably was not legitimate, but it saved me bucks and they felt sorry for the nice little lady building her own house.

After working with someone for a time, you begin to understand their pattern. A couple of the workers were always a few days late. If I asked them to come on Wednesday, they would say, *"of course"* and show up on

Friday. If I really needed them on Wednesday, then I would ask them to be there on Monday. It worked perfectly. Final inspection was creeping up. It had been seven tedious months. Most homes, built by experts, are completed in three. I was anxious to sell the trailer and sleep in a real bed. I was getting claustrophobic and I needed a long ten-minute hot shower.

Mr. Harris was installing my heating and air conditioning system and was one of those who was always late – sometimes a week or more. He had completed the major installation and had a few things to finalize, but some other work by other contractors needed to be finished first. He had asked me to give him a call when I was ready. I called. Mr. Harris, a middle-aged, slow talking, slight man, said he'd be there the following day. I was ecstatic. Finishing up the heating and air was the last item before I could call for final inspection.

The following day Mr. Harris didn't show. I was disappointed, but not surprised. He didn't show the next day. I was still not surprised. I called to sweetly remind him of our appointment. I regurgitated sugar and spice and everything nice.

"Kathy," he said sincerely, "you are the nicest person I have ever worked for."

"Thank you," I responded and then in my finest joking voice, "but then why can't you be here on time? I can be a real bitch if that's what it takes."

Mr. Harris laughed and said, "I'll be tomorrow...for

sure."

He arrived on time, finished his work and I called the county offices. The county inspector arrived two days later and an hour passed the appointed time. Nervously I followed him around the structure answering questions and playing my sweet-lady card again. He ignored the cot I had placed in one of the bedrooms. One was forbidden to occupy a structure until after final inspection. I told him I was just storing the cot there along with some blankets. He smirked. He had been to the house before on previous scheduled inspections and was pleased to discover all discrepancies had been fixed or completed.

"You need to pave the driveway before I can sign you off," he said.

I was tired. I was tired of living in a trailer. I was tired of taking showers at work. I was tired of this project. I cried.

"I'm out of money," I whimpered, "I need to sell the trailer before I can pave the driveway."

He sighed, "Okay, I guess I can make an exception. I'll let you slide."

"Thank you," I sniveled.

"Promise me you'll get it done," he frowned.

I promised and I did. It was two months later, but I got it done.

Good Reason To Be Late

I finally did it. It took several years of managing work, Karen and classes, but I finally was receiving my degree in supervision from San Diego Mesa College. The company ran a column each June in the *News Meter*, the employee's monthly newsletter, commemorating college graduates.

In the *News Meter* was a monthly column, *What Next?* by Don Everberg, featuring bits and pieces of personal stuff about employees and their families. In the June, 1984 issue I was mentioned – not because of anything wonderful I had done, but because the company was slow to adjust to women in the workplace...*very slow*. Don reported:

"GOOD REASON TO BE LATE: Kathy, Miramar Storage Yard, was slow sending her picture to *News Meter* in connection with a degree she received from Mesa Evening College. She hadn't known about the annual graduates' issue, because she didn't see the notice. It was on the bulletin board in the men's lavatory. We're hoping for wider distribution of future notices."

Wish I'd Had a Camera

He was short, thin, had a receding hairline, was conniving and had twenty-three Snoopy toys on his desk - not counting the Snoopy coffee mug and the Snoopy magnets on his file cabinet. He was my boss. Geoff Simon was the Material Distribution Supervisor at the Miramar location.

It was 1985 and I was in my third year as Material Distribution Foreman. I had determined that Miramar was the company asylum. I wondered why I had been sent there.

Geoff was a blabbermouth. One did not tell Geoff any personal secrets. One did not tell Geoff any company secrets. One did not tell Geoff much of anything. But it was fun to have a secret about Geoff.

I can understand someone having a passion for a cartoon character. But as he added to his collection, it appeared to be a psychotic obsession. The employees found it challenging to stand before him and receive instructions or reprimands in the audience of a multitude of inanimate flop-eared dogs.

I had purchased a four-foot-tall inflatable Snoopy Santa several years before I met Geoff. After being inflated, deflated, stored for eleven months and the process repeated numerous times, my Snoopy developed a slow leak. I couldn't fine the offending minuscule puncture, so in early December I decided to donate my Snoopy to Geoff's collection. He was ecstatic. I informed him about the leak.

Geoff inflated the dog-doll to see if he could determine where the problem was. The inflated Snoopy was in Geoff's

196

office. The pumped-up Snoop slowly began to sag. Geoff blew him up again. This was an embarrassing position as I had discovered when I owned Snoopy. His valve stem was located on his tummy. Geoff decided to see if he could feel and hear the air escaping. A person's cheek is very sensitive and a good natural monitoring device for infinitely slight breezes. I walked in on Geoff in a compromising position. The four-foot Snoopy was sitting on the guest chair with his perpetual smile and Geoff was on his knees with his head between Snoopy's legs.

"I know you like Snoopy," I grinned, "but this is taking it a little too far."

Geoff became aware of the situation's appearance and leaped to his feet, stumbling in his panic.

"I'm looking for his leak," he stammered red-faced and embarrassed.

"No, don't mind me," I smirked, "finish what you were doing. I'll be back later."

I quietly chuckled. By the time I got back to my desk my eyes were filled with the tears of silent laughter. I wish I'd had a camera.

Power Withheld

Being promoted to Material Distribution Foreman, a first rung on the corporate ladder, my responsibilities included the truck drivers, scheduling deliveries and pick-ups, and working closely with the Material Control Department. We were all under the same corporate umbrella. Material Control was responsible for keeping the inventory at an appropriate level. Most of these employees were above me on the corporate ladder by several rungs. Two of these "gentlemen," Albert - the guys called him Alburp - and Sheldon - Sheldumb - were close friends with my immediate boss, Geoff Simon - Simple Simon. I wondered what the guys called me but decided I really didn't want to know.

Occasionally Albert, Geoff and Sheldon would visit the outlying districts to check the stock on hand. Sometimes it was necessary, but most of the time it was just an excuse to get out of the office for a couple of hours. On one of these trips I invited myself to ride along with Albert. I needed to discuss some concerns with the supervisor at a district warehouse.

Albert was seven years older than me, always dressed in a blue suit and tie and carried a brief case that seemed permanently attached to his hand. He was married, had a couple of teenagers and talked about them continuously. He was just over six-feet with a paunch and thick greasy fifties-style hair. A stomach problem caused him to burp frequently – Alburp.

DO THESE WORK BOOTS MAKE MY FEET LOOK FAT?

Kathleen McLaughlin

I grabbed a clipboard, paper and pencil and climbed in the company car where Albert was waiting. He smiled. He was a little creepy, but I looked forward to the opportunity to visit with the district supervisor and do something besides deskwork. Within a few minutes, I rolled down the passenger window after carefully considering the cool autumn weather and my girly coiffure. I had come to the realization that Albert only owned one blue suit and wore it daily. Albert reeked of body odor. It became a long twenty-one mile drive to Eastern Operating District.

At Eastern we met with the supervisor, wandered around the facility and made some useless notes. We ate lunch from the vending machines due to Albert's lack of cash and my unwillingness to foot the bill at a café. I had been warned by Sheldon and Geoff of Albert's lack of money at opportune times. As we headed back to our home base, Albert took an unexpected turn off the freeway onto a main road that leads though La Mesa.

"Where are we going?" I asked.

"Oh, I just want to check on the apartment," Albert replied.

I became uneasy, but Albert had never made any advances toward me in the past so I inquired about the apartment. I knew he and his family lived in north county about thirty miles away. I assumed he owned some rental units. As we drove into the parking lot of a multi-unit apartment complex on Lake Murray Drive, Albert explained, "Sheldon, Geoff and I share the rent on this apartment."

"You mean you're partners in this apartment building?" I asked being impressed.

"Hell, no. We just use one apartment for 'special' occasions," he said with a sneer and a wink. I sighed and wondered if I was going to have to take this fat smelly guy out with one swift kick.

He parked the car and told me to wait. He said he'd be right back. I was relieved. The "special" occasion this afternoon must not have been me – thank goodness. In a few minutes, Albert returned, started the car and we headed again to Miramar. Making idol conversation and trying to avoid an awkward situation, I asked if everything seemed to be okay.

Albert smirked, "I had the place yesterday. Geoff's got it this afternoon. I was just checking to see if I left it clean enough."

Leaning my head toward the open car window, I enjoyed the refreshing breeze. Albert's rotten moral fiber suddenly made him smell even worse.

Back at my office, I finished some paperwork - there's always paperwork - and headed for my little truck at the end of the day. I chose not to regurgitate any pleasant acknowledgments like "see you tomorrow" or "have a nice day" to my fellow employees. They didn't seem to notice. I pondered the intelligence of Albert's letting me in on the trios' dirty-little-secret. Each member of the triad was married – happily, or so I thought. Geoff had a new grandbaby. I wondered what their wives ever saw in any of them. They not only were cheating on their families, but doing it on company time. The wicked Kathy within thought briefly of blackmail, but, the angel on my other shoulder said, "no." It was amusing to consider. Geoff drove up in the company car returning from his "business" meeting in La Mesa. He stopped and got out.

"Wait up, Kathy," he shouted.

I paused; after all, he was my boss. The short, thin man wheezed and gasped nervously as he stammered, "There's no need to say anything about that place."

"What place?" I asked in a monotone.

"You know. Albert told me you had stopped by that place. There's no need to mention it, is there?"

"What place?" I repeated, turned and climbed in my LUV truck. He stood with a forced smile and shoulders drooped. I felt some unexplained pity for the pathetic wimp. I drove home looking forward to seeing my daughter.

San Diego Women's Foreman Association

Being a woman foreman with twenty-one men reporting to me was daunting. Everyday frustrations of men finding excuses not to do what was instructed had my nails bitten down to the quick.

Most duties at the Miramar warehouse and storage yard were dictated by the volume of material and supplies ordered by the various districts. It was the extracurricular projects that I found difficult. I had to find a way to make the work "their idea." I would ask if anyone had any thoughts on how to organize the pole-mount transformers or what we could do about empty pallets that had been left abandoned here and there around the thirteen acres. The men were more efficient if they thought it was their idea. I made suggestions and inquired as to their opinion. It worked. But the frustration in getting things accomplished was taking its toll.

At SDGE in the mid 1980's only three women sported the title of foreman. Mary worked in the company's transformer repair department in Kearny Mesa. Brooke worked in the test laboratory located at Tenth and Imperial Avenues downtown. One of us - I don't remember who - decided that maybe we should get together for lunch. The timing was right. We met at a central location.

The luncheon went great. We talked about our job responsibilities, joked about issues with our bosses and laughed about co-workers. We discovered that many of our issues were identical. We all had bosses who explained assignments to us as if we were children. We all determined that we each had to work twice as hard as the men. We joked about having to motivate our subordinates to perform the duties they had been hired for. We chuckled. It was wonderful. I returned to the office with a new outlook, a smile on my face, and frustrations vented.

Thus was the beginning of the San Diego Women's Foreman Association, an "official" organization, or at least that was the perception of our bosses. Every couple of months, our support group - all three of us - joined together to have official meetings - aka venting lunches.

Nothing Changes

Discrimination has always been an issue. I'm going to guess that cavemen discriminated against other cavemen for who-knows-why. Back in the early sixties, the term "affirmative action" became popular. The expression was used as an attempt to create equal rights based on race, religion, national origin and eventually gender. But, of course, a piece of paper cannot change the minds of those with brains locked in a metal vault.

The Civil Rights Act of 1964 was supposed to outlaw forms of discrimination against blacks and women. The law was basically weak, but at least it was a beginning. Ongoing forms of bigotry against groups and individuals still disgustingly continue. During the seventies we fought for the Equal Rights Amendment (ERA). Even in 1776, Abigail Adams wrote to her husband John, "remember the ladies and do not put such unlimited power into the hands of the husbands." He just laughed, much the same as men do today.

In 1972, Title IX of the Education Amendments was introduced. In an early draft, there was little mention of athletics and the focus was more specifically to provide women with an equal chance to attend the schools of their choice, to develop the skills they want and to have a fair chance at obtaining the job of their choice with equal pay. They - meaning the media - got hold of the sports aspect of Title IX and it received some skewed publicity. But, it has made a difference for today's young women even if it took

40 years.

Several events took place during the 80's which I decided were noteworthy. Why else would I have saved theses news clipping all these years?

In *The San Diego Union*, on Wednesday, May 7, 1980: a nearly full-page article about my book, *"My Mom, The Truck Driver."* The article, by Greg Joseph, emphasized the positive side of the book. "Still, this attractive, tawny-haired mother of one has gamely confronted the problems head-on, attaching the prejudices of traditional social stereotyping with a wry sense of humor and an irrepressible, can't-win-'em-all attitude." I liked the "attractive" part the best.

In *The San Diego Union* on Friday, June 11, 1982 a small article appeared announcing the California State Senate voted to "boost the penalty for employers who pay unequal wages to men and women for equal work." The penalty rose from 30 days jail time and a $50 fine to six months jail time and a $10,000 fine, making the state penalties the same as the federal government. About time! Too bad they don't enforce it.

On June 11, 1982 the *San Diego Union* reported that Atwater, CA set a record with a KC-135 tanker (big plane) as "the first-ever all-woman crew took off from Castle Air Force Base." The article also added that all three ground support members and two schedulers were women. If this were on Facebook I'd give them a "Like." Thumbs up!

In *Parade Magazine* on August 4, 1985 the article entitled "The World of Women" featured two scholarly reports:

World Feminization of Poverty by Rosemary Sarri of the University of Michigan's School of Social Work, and *Women... A World Survey* by Ruth Leger Sivard of World Priorities, a research organization based in Washington, DC. Sarri disclosed that "while women comprise more than half of the world's population and labor more than two-thirds of its work-time, they own less than 1% of its property and earn only 10% of its income." Sivard stated that "There is no major field of activity and no country where women have attained equality with men." They did say that education is the area where women have made the most strides. In 1950, there were 95 million females enrolled in school and in 1985, there were 390 million.

In *The Wall Street Journal* on March 24, 1986 appeared *A Special Report: The Corporate Woman*. This special twenty-eight page insert reported on problems like the "Glass Ceiling." The articles reiterated issues women were having at the upper rungs of the corporate ladder. Many men did not feel comfortable with a woman in the room. Some top executives were "too quick to feel the woman who is tough isn't being womanly, while the woman who isn't tough isn't worth having around." These feelings seem to have remained over the decades. Another of the articles stated "nearly one in five (men) felt that women are 'temperamentally unfit' for management." Interesting, I guess men aren't temperamental.

I had to laugh when I read an account of a woman executive chairing a meeting at a huge corporation - one

206

founded in 1911, and it is still around. The financial managers kept addressing her male subordinates for answers she could only provide. The subordinates would then have to turn to her for the information.

Many of the corporate women who felt stuck under glass left those "manly" businesses to start their own companies. When their organizations became successful I'm sure a "neener, neener, neener" was in order.

Unfortunately, law suits appear to be the only way to get anything accomplished. I wished I had been the suing kind. I would be filthy rich by now.

In 1987 *The Wall Street Journal* featured *The Pioneers: Women Who Fought Sex Bias on the Job Prove To Be a Varied Group*. This article discussed law-suits that ranged from women who in 1969 were denied jobs because of a "state labor rule barring women from jobs that involved lifting more than 30 pounds – about the weight of an average two-year-old – made a promotion impossible." A union representative said he didn't want women in physical jobs because men are the "bread winners." Tell that to all the single moms. Stories about a woman who could not be a guard at a prison because she did not weigh enough or another about a flight attendant who was fired for being married left me wondering if things would ever progress.

The ERA has lost national attention and center stage. The universal sentiment is that we operate in an "equal" world. Women have been struggling for equal rights in this country since the beginning and still are especially when a dean from a major university makes snide remarks about women and math and science. Abigail Adams, Elizabeth Cady Stanton, Lucretia Mott, Susan B. Anthony, Sojourner Truth, Alice Paul are only a few of our histories fighters. After forty years, The National Council of Women's Organizations is still pressing on to have the ERA passed as the 28th Amendment to the Constitution. I hope they are successful.

It was not considered socially acceptable for women during the Great Depression to have a job. After all, men were the breadwinners. Enterprising women started their own businesses selling baked goods, eggs, cheese or other home-made products or services.

After WWII, many women were forced to give-up their jobs to the returning veterans, even if their husband was not fortunate enough to come home. Many of these women became entrepreneurs.

The recession of the 1970's again found women losing jobs due to nationwide "lay-offs." Business ownership was, again, an option. Unfortunately, recessions happen every thirty years or so. The recession that began in 2008 resulted in many male-dominated industries to cutback employees. Women, once more, became the principal breadwinners. The popularity of internet and social media has been a huge boost in small home-grown enterprises for women entrepreneurs, even though about 72% of women still work outside the home. But more of them hold management positions.

We haven't made much progress with the wage gap. Men still make more than women performing the same job. And, in 2012, only a tad more than 3% of public traded companies had a woman CEO.

In 2013, women are graduating from college at approximately the same rate as men. Women are earning more than half of master, doctoral and professional degrees. Hooray!

Progress moves very slowly. Changes in lending laws, like the Equal Credit Act of the 1970's, have allowed women to obtain the capital needed to start a business. Even though I had a lucrative, steady job with SDG&E, in 1974, I was denied a loan for a house Karen and I loved. I was not aware of the recent passing of the law. And again, too bad I'm not the suing kind. I would be filthy rich by now.

I will end with one of my favorite quotes from many many many years ago:

"Nothing can be more absurd than the practice which prevails in our country of men and women not following the same pursuits with all their strengths and with one mind – for thus the state, instead of being whole, is reduced to a half." ~ Plato: (428 BC – 347 BC) Greek philosopher, mathematician and obviously a very smart guy!

Made in the USA
San Bernardino, CA
18 February 2014